Measuring the Success of Organization Development

A Step-by-Step Guide to Measuring Impact and Calculating ROI

ROI INSTITUTE™

Patricia Pulliam Phillips, PhD
Jack J. Phillips, PhD
Lizette Zuniga, PhD

16 15 14 13 1 2 3 4 5

ASTD Press is an internationally renowned source of insightful and practical information on workplace learning, performance, and professional development.

ASTD Press
1640 King Street Box 1443
Alexandria, VA 22313-1443 USA

Ordering information: Books published by ASTD Press can be purchased by visiting ASTD's website at store.astd.org or by calling 800.628.2783 or 703.683.8100.

Library of Congress Control Number: 2013931624
ISBN-10: 1-56286-873-X
ISNB-13: 978-1-56286-873-4
e-ISBN: 978-1-60728-521-2

ASTD Press Editorial Staff:
Director: Glenn Saltzman
Manager and Editor, ASTD Press: Ashley McDonald
Community of Practice Manager, Senior Leaders & Executives: Nancy Olson
Editorial Assistant: Sarah Cough
Text Design: Natasha van de Graaff
Cover Design: Ana Foreman

Printed by Versa Press, Inc., East Peoria, IL, www.versapress.com

Table of Contents

Preface v

Part I: The ROI Methodology: A Credible Approach to Evaluating Your OD Interventions 1

Chapter 1 Organization Development: The Basics 3
What Is OD? 4
Glossary of OD Terms 8
Common Pitfalls of OD Projects: Lessons Learned 13
Current Challenges for OD 23
Final Thoughts 25

Chapter 2 Developing a Measurement Culture 27
Leadership and Culture 28
High-Performing Culture 28
How and Why OD Fits With ROI 31
OD and the ROI Methodology 32
Final Thoughts 40

Chapter 3 Alignment and Evaluation Planning 41
Selecting Interventions for ROI Analysis 41
Integrating Diagnostics With the ROI Methodology 45
Aligning OD Projects With the Business 46
Evaluation Planning 54
Case Study 55
Final Thoughts 57

Chapter 4 Data Collection 61
Quantitative and Qualitative Inquiry 61
Data Collection Methods 63
Sources of Data 73
Timing for Data Collection 75
Final Thoughts 77

Chapter 5 Data Analysis . . . 79
Isolating the Effects . . . 79
Converting Data to Monetary Units . . . 86
Calculating the Return . . . 92
Costs of the Intervention . . . 95
Final Thoughts . . . 100

Chapter 6 Communicating Results . . . 101
The Dos of Communicating Results . . . 102
The Don'ts of Communicating Results . . . 104
The Report Formula . . . 105
The Communication Plan . . . 111
Final Thoughts . . . 112

Chapter 7 Implementing and Sustaining ROI . . . 113
The Importance of Sustaining the Use of ROI . . . 113
Implementing the Process: Overcoming Resistance . . . 114
Developing Roles and Responsibilities . . . 116
Establishing Goals and Plans . . . 118
Initiating ROI Studies . . . 122
Final Thoughts . . . 126

Part II: Evaluation in Action: Case Studies Describing the Evaluation of OD Interventions . . . 129

Chapter 8 Organization Culture Change . . . 131
Lizette Zuniga, PhD

Chapter 9 Stress Management in Teams . . . 149
Jack J. Phillips, PhD, and Patti P. Phillips, PhD

Chapter 10 Organizational Change . . . 175
Holly Burkett, PhD, SPHR, CPT

References . . . 197
About the ROI Institute . . . 200
About the Authors . . . 201
Index . . . 203

Preface

The fluctuation that has occurred worldwide economically and politically has caused organizations to adjust to new global and environmental challenges. Likewise, the field of organization development (OD) has had to adapt at an increasingly rapid rate. With resources being challenged, the question is raised as to whether OD interventions show value. This question is being asked repeatedly and increasingly. To understand what it means to apply measurement to organization development, OD practitioners need to develop both a base of measurement skills and an understanding of critical elements foundational to aligning interventions with what matters most.

This book came from seeing a gap in our field. We have interacted with a number of OD practitioners and have noted several consistent themes from those conversations:

- The way we approach business is changing at a rate we are unaccustomed to.
- OD interventions are pointedly lacking in measurement and evaluation.
- Paradoxically, OD practitioners are increasingly being asked to measure and evaluate, showing the value of their work.
- OD practitioners lack the necessary knowledge and skills to measure results in a consistent and credible way.

There are literally thousands of books on improving organizations and leadership. There are also many books on measurement and evaluation, yet in our research, we have found very few that marry the topics of OD and evaluation in a credible and easy-to-use manner. This book addresses that gap. Our work in applying the ROI Methodology has set the stage for clear and practical implementation. This is not a book about quick fixes; it is embedded in reality, in everyday practice and application. It is not written for theory's sake; it is written to bring about long-term and sustainable change in the workplace, while raising the bar of accountability. *Measuring the Success of Organization Development* is written with C-suite, stakeholders, leaders, OD practitioners, HR professionals, and evaluators in mind.

We aren't claiming that this book has everything, but we do believe that it lays a strong foundation for implementing the ROI Methodology to OD interventions. This book contains real examples with real challenges and real answers. Our goal is to help today's professional align interventions with what is most important, to conduct diagnostics and needs assessment with the end in mind, and to use a simple 10-step model to showcase results.

We have attempted to write a book that is both interesting and user-friendly. There are a number of examples throughout the book, illustrating the use of the ROI Methodology to OD interventions. Three case studies (chapters 8, 9, and 10) demonstrate the application of the ROI process to OD interventions.

We see the field of OD and ROI as fertile ground, rich with potential. What we hope to see is that others take the challenge, apply the methodology to different types of OD interventions, and then turn around and share their successes and lessons learned. The OD community, in this regard, grows as a learning entity, deepening its knowledge and skills, while continuing to contribute to its body of knowledge.

HOW THIS BOOK IS ORGANIZED

This book plots a course to bring accountability to OD. It shows how to measure the effectiveness in ways that all involved in OD interventions will recognize, appreciate, and ultimately need. The first chapter sets the stage by defining terms and identifying common pitfalls, presenting challenges for the OD field and a forecast of what's in store for OD. The next chapter is about organization culture and building a measurement culture. In this chapter, the ROI Methodology is introduced and its connection to OD is established. The issues of business alignment and planning for measurement and evaluation are explored next. One of the key issues is connecting OD directly to the organization before, during, and after the interventions take place. The next few chapters represent the heart of the ROI Methodology, showing how data are collected, analyzed, and reported to various audiences. Following that, the book details the ways in which this methodology can be sustained over a long period of time. Finally, the book concludes with three case studies, illustrating how the ROI process is used with OD interventions.

As always, we welcome your comments and feedback. Please contact us via email at info@roiinstitute.net.

Patti Phillips, PhD
Jack Phillips, PhD
Lizette Zuniga, PhD

Part I

ROI Methodology

A Credible Approach to Evaluating Your OD Interventions

1

Organization Development: The Basics

There are no secrets to success. It is the result of preparation, hard work, and learning from failure.

—Colin Powell

The discovery of the New World by Christopher Columbus in 1492 is a classic example of the clash between two different cultures. The two groups of people were of completely different backgrounds, and yet they found a way to communicate with each other by exchanging food and gifts. In his diary, Columbus classified the Native Americans as Neolithic and primitive; whereas the Spaniards, in his mind, represented the latest in progress and civilization. Columbus planned to return to Spain and give a report to the king and queen. Before leaving, he built a fortress on the island and left behind 43 sailors to demonstrate the intent to conquer and dominate the land. When Columbus returned to the island from Spain, he discovered that the 43 men he left behind were now dead. He also found out that the Spaniards he left behind had taken the Native American women by force, which led to retaliation from the Native Americans, by taking the lives of the Spaniards. Neither group of people really understood each other or their motives. Minimal effort was made to understand each other's values or ways of living. Columbus and his group of Spaniards were motivated by power and conquest, and the Native Americans responded with fear and protectiveness.

The story of Christopher Columbus discovering America has been told many different ways, providing evidence of the impact of culture and change. For our purposes in understanding organizational development (OD), this story illustrates the complexities of groups of people, different perspectives, and the messiness associated with change. Change is the hallmark of OD. An OD practitioner knows that change does not happen all of a sudden. There is usually someone or a group of people planning and driving the change. Often, organizational change happens by mistake, in the midst of day-to-day business; but it can result in strong reactions, defensiveness, and clashes between different groups of people. The results are sometimes quite different than expected. The practitioner has the challenge of planning the change, selecting the right method to evoke change, looking for ways to make change stick and then, determining whether the intervention is effective. Many resources are available that describe how to plan and evoke change; and even more in sustaining processes that help us manage. This book focuses on the latter—measuring the effectiveness of change initiatives and the extent to which they drive results, reaping a positive return on investment (ROI). But before we get into the content on measurement, it is important to build a foundation.

WHAT IS OD?

Organization development, abbreviated as OD, is a planned intervention of change focused on groups of people, teams, departments, or organizations with the purpose of organization improvement, drawing from disciplines of applied behavioral science, industrial/organization psychology, anthropology, and social systems. Bennis (1969) defines organization development this way:

> *A response to change, a complex educational strategy intended to change the beliefs, attitudes, values, and structure of organizations so that they can better adapt to new technologies, markets, and challenges at the dizzying rate of change itself.*

OD is a field of practice that focuses on individual development, team or group development, as well as development of the organization itself. By focusing on the group, and its unique characteristics, this effort often leads to affecting the organization. Usually, the topic of OD includes a discussion of organization culture as a critical component to the practice of OD. Organization culture is briefly defined later in this chapter and will be explored in more depth in chapter 2, particularly as it relates to measurement and evaluation.

Types of organization development interventions include the following:

- change management
- leadership development
- team development
- coaching
- 360-degree feedback
- strategic planning
- organization design and structure
- succession planning
- mentoring
- performance management
- merger cultural integration
- individual, team, or organization assessment
- training and learning.

Making the Business Case for OD

Organizations are changing at an increasing rate. Among other things, the economy and technology are driving serious change in the workplace. Regardless of the type of organization, industry, product, service, or customers it serves, innovation and organization agility are requirements for survival in today's marketplace. Leaders must function differently and organizations must be set up distinctly to maximize their business efforts and adapt to change more readily.

The 2012 Annual Global CEO Survey, conducted by PricewaterhouseCoopers International, revealed relevant findings for making the business case for OD:

- Of the CEOs responding, 56 percent indicated they plan to have new business models.
- Also, 55 percent indicated they plan to change existing products and services.
- One in three responded they were concerned about skills shortages that will affect their company's ability to innovate effectively.
- Productivity and labor costs were identified as critical measures, yet CEOs indicated they need more information on the effectiveness of their investments in talent.

Ongoing concerns for CEOs include workforces being effective and productive. Indicators of increasing importance are morale, job satisfaction, process improvement, and quality of work. To this end, OD plays a significant role in navigating change in organizations, developing leadership, and structuring organizations to be more flexible for the changing needs of the marketplace.

In consideration of best practices, most of the Fortune 500 organizations have OD teams or departments. The OD function helps organizations assess themselves and their work environments, identify strategic priorities, and get back on track when needed. OD diagnoses the areas where help is most needed; and in large-scale change projects, it paves the way for change management. Ultimately, OD is the vehicle for organizations to be flexible and pliable to the ever-changing needs of the market.

The OD Process

Action research is the hallmark of the OD process. In the 1950s, Kurt Lewin described the process in which data were used to drive change in terms of planning, action, and measuring results. These steps were repeated until the desired change took place. Lewin's three main steps are:

1. **Unfreezing:** the step where motivation for change is created and awareness for the need for change is identified. Whether it's an individual, group, or organization, there is usually some sort of gap between the current state and the ideal state. Without tapping into motivation and need for change, receptivity to

change will not be present. Resistance to change must be addressed.

> **Case in Point**
> 360-degree feedback shows that frontline supervisors need to develop more business acumen to be poised for promotion within their organization. The unfreezing phase in this example shows the business acumen gap and lays a strong foundation for why the change is needed.

2. **Changing or Movement:** diagnosis is made, solutions are identified, and new behavior is tested to make changes toward an ideal state.

> **Case in Point**
> Using the same example, the frontline supervisors engage in activities to increase business acumen. The supervisors enroll in a twofold initiative; one is an online learning module and the other is mentoring. The idea is that they actively participate in the change process and increase their business acumen.

3. **Refreezing:** change happens in this step with behaviors implemented and reinforced until they become habitual. Something needs to happen in the organization for the change to take hold. Unfortunately, this step is often overlooked. Just because change is introduced does not mean that the change is permanent. To refreeze implies that the OD practitioner identifies and builds into the change management plans how change will be sustained.

> **Case in Point**
> Continuing with our frontline supervisor example, the frontline supervisors not only increase their business acumen but they begin to show knowledge in their jobs. They begin to work on projects where they are called upon to use said business acumen.

The phases that Lewin identified were foundational for the field of OD. Of course, the process is broken down into more specific steps. While OD practitioners use variations of steps followed, Table 1-1 illustrates a common set of steps involved in the OD process.

TABLE 1-1. OD Process

Step	Description
Preliminary assessment	This step involves conducting a mini-assessment identifying initial concerns, observed dynamics, etc. This phase leads to the formation of a hypothesis. It normally takes place in the initial meeting with the client, when the OD practitioner assesses the readiness for change, as well as a preliminary analysis around what it will take to foster change.
Data gathering	The next step tests the hypothesis through the process of collecting data. This usually leads to understanding the deeper issues and diagnosing the main problems. This step generally employs the use of interviews, questionnaires, organization records, focus groups, and other types of data collection methods.
Feedback of findings	Once data are gathered, analysis proceeds. This step is focused on providing feedback. Emphasis is on sharing findings in a non-threatening atmosphere and engaging the leaders/clients through a collaborative discussion of the findings.
Joint action planning	This is the step in which awareness is raised and problems are identified. As problems are acknowledged, solutions are explored. The OD practitioner actively works with the client/client group and together they decide the best course of action to take.
OD intervention	The OD intervention is implemented. The OD practitioner may be directly involved in facilitating the intervention or may involve others to intervene.
Preliminary evaluation	This step is to understand whether the intervention is working or needs modification.
Modification	If the preliminary evaluation shows that modification is needed, then this step is included.
Measuring results	This step is aimed at determining whether the intervention is yielding the desired results, or the ideal state.

The steps outlined in Table 1-1 show how the OD process is data driven. Action research emphasizes collecting data and using data to drive diagnosis and interventions. Data are used to facilitate discussions with clients, to raise awareness of the greatest needs, and to measure the results of the intervention.

Case in Point

An OD practitioner uses the outcomes from an organizational culture assessment to measure domains of planning, leadership, values, decision making, and structure to help understand the culture and to prioritize the needs in the organization. In this case, the instrument is used to help understand and diagnose problem areas. The organization scores lower in the planning domain, revealing the absence of planning and prioritizing what was important for the business. So the OD practitioner takes this input and holds discussions with key stakeholders and together, they decide the best step to take is to hold strategic planning sessions, which will help the organization not only determine short- and long-term plans, but will also help prioritize for employees what is most important. To determine whether the strategic planning sessions made the difference for the organization, measures are put into place to determine whether the gap is closed.

Most fields have their own language and OD is no exception. In the next section, we provide some of the common words that make up the work of OD practitioners along with some definitions and examples.

GLOSSARY OF OD TERMS

The increasing body of literature in the field of OD shows there is not unanimous agreement on the meaning of all of the terms; however, there is a need to provide general definitions. These descriptions, along with key features, will provide understanding and context as we apply measurement and evaluation to OD.

Organization Effectiveness

Historically, organization effectiveness was defined by how well an organization performed on a variety of metrics, examining different parts of the organization, and measuring indicators connected with productivity and internal processes. Examples of these measures are:

- how quickly products were brought to market
- whether an organization was a place of best practice
- attracting the right talent
- how they stacked up against competition.

Today, organization effectiveness theorists have expanded criteria for measuring the effectiveness of an organization to include other aspects of organization characteristics. These include flexibility, open communication, retention, creativity, growth, satisfaction, and efficiencies.

The idea here is that assessing organization effectiveness means understanding and measuring organizational goals and strategies. Why does the organization exist? What does the organization plan to achieve? Organization effectiveness has become increasingly important, as there is a more explicit focus on business impact and bottom-line results.

Change Management

James Belasco, in his book *Teaching the Elephant to Dance* (1990), uses the metaphor of young elephants being trained through the use of heavy shackles so when they are older, they will stay in place. Of course, when they are older, they are powerful and could easily break loose, but because of their conditioning, they stay put. This metaphor is relevant for the subject of change management because organizations have learned to do things a certain way and to unlearn habits is a slow and arduous process.

The simplest definition for change is *doing things differently or doing different things*. When someone wants to lose weight, they usually eat less (doing something differently), and they may also start an exercise program (doing different things). The change effort has a plan in place based on specific objectives, which are derived from diagnostics or a needs assessment. What is the desired state? Recognizing the desired state, understanding the current state, and defining the gap leads to developing specific objectives.

Research from Prosci in 2007 showed that when the change management component of a project was rated as excellent, 88 percent of projects met or exceeded objectives. Conversely, when change management was rated as poor, 83 percent of projects failed to meet objectives and deadlines (*The Portland Business Journal*, 2008).

Case in Point

A cellular phone company based in the United States had plans to implement a new software system to help manage and expedite billing and accounting. The organization developed a very tedious and complex plan to migrate to the new software system. IT consultants were brought on board and additional staff was hired to help with the process. Unfortunately, the plan did not include change management and consequently, the system implementation resulted in increased customer complaints and losses of more than $2 million from billing inaccuracies in the first six months.

Similar to Lewin, Prosci (1996) outlines three phases to manage change.

1. **Prepare for change:** This phase is about getting ready for change and raising awareness about what is involved to achieve change goals. Included in this phase are defining the strategy for change management, preparing the members of the change management team, and developing a sponsorship model.

2. **Manage change:** The main emphasis of this phase is to create plans to execute the change management project. This phase involves developing change management plans and taking actions to implement plans.

3. **Reinforce change:** The focus of this phase is sustaining the change. Steps are taken to collect and analyze feedback, diagnose the gaps, manage resistance, and implement corrective actions along the way while celebrating successes.

In what ways do organizations need to adapt and learn? What new skills and knowledge does an organization need to continue to grow and improve? In what ways does an organization need to create processes to share information so employees can do their jobs better? In what ways does an organization benefit from sharing lessons learned? These types of questions lead us to our next term: organization learning.

Organization Learning

The term *organization learning* was first coined by Cyart and March (1963) and became popular almost immediately in the business world. The process of organization learning enables organizations to manage change and share knowledge in order to achieve strategic goals. Organization learning allows the right hand to know what the left hand is doing, so to speak. Clarity and connecting the dots are part of this process.

It's hard to talk about organization learning without mentioning the term *learning organization*, which was made popular by Peter Senge (1990). In The *Fifth Discipline*, Senge defines learning organizations as those organizations where people continually expand their capacity to achieve desired results, where innovative thoughts are reinforced, and where groups within the organization continually learn and grow. Senge was describing an ideal organization. In a learning organization, mistakes are shared for the benefit of lessons learned. This can sometimes lead to something better than what would have been, had the mistake not been made.

At the core of organization learning is how an organization thinks and reacts. Organization learning goes hand in hand with our next term, *organization culture*.

Organization Culture

It's hard to use words sparingly when describing organization culture. This is a complicated term that has not been easy to define. Schein himself admitted this complexity (2010). Organization culture has layers and depth involving what is apparent and obvious as well as unseen and subtle. It's more about the *how* than the *what*; the focus is on how work is approached rather than what is produced.

Case in Point

The story of Post-it® notes illustrates this concept very well. Spencer Silver was working in the 3M research labs in the 1970s and was trying to find a strong adhesive. Instead, the one he created was weaker than the one they had. No one knew what to do with the product, but still, they decided not to ditch it. Four years went by when another scientist, Arthur Fry, was singing in his church choir and wanted placeholders in his hymnal. He remembered the product made by Silver. By 1980, the unplanned product, Post-it notes, were available for distribution. The 3M company had a 15 percent rule that allowed employees to spend 15 percent of their time on exploring and developing new ideas and fostering innovation. The glue on the back of the paper was a "mistake"; but instead of canning it, the organization decided to see the mistake through to the end. Today, this unplanned product is one of the most popular office products available.

There are various domains that have been included when understanding and measuring organization culture. Beard and Zuniga (2006) included domains of leadership, planning, and decision making in their instrument, "Capstone Organization Culture Survey." Dennison, in his "Organization Culture Survey," measures aspects of leadership and planning as well as other factors. While chapter 2 of this book is dedicated to this subject in more depth, we recognize it as part of the OD glossary and offer a definition written by Goffee and Jones (1998):

> *Culture comes down to a common way of thinking, which derives a common way of acting on the job, or producing a product in a factory. Usually these shared assumptions, beliefs, and values are unspoken, implicit.*

Culture in this sense is not to be confused with national culture. While national culture plays a role in influencing the way business is conducted, the focus of organization culture is on the organization itself.

Up to this point, we have used the term *OD practitioners* but we have not fully described this professional, or the required competence to be an OD practitioner; that is described next.

Case in Point

For example, the way Southwest Airlines approaches their work stems from the way the original CEO, Herb Kelleher, set into motion a relaxed atmosphere that places high value on its employees and encourages them to have fun at work. CEO Gary Kelly, who viewed the people as the airline's "greatest competitive weapon," further reinforced this environment. They may fly the same Boeing model, hand out the same type of snack, and follow the same FAA regulations as their competitors, but the culture is unique to Southwest when compared to some of the airlines that are categorically more traditional. Southwest has enjoyed its profitability for 35 consecutive years and has grown into the world's third largest airline. While revenues have slowed recently, they have maintained their focus on the workforce.

OD Practitioners

While there is a mix of backgrounds among OD practitioners, by and large, OD professionals are those who carry out the OD function. Some are internal to their organizations and some are external consultants; in either case, they provide OD services to organizations. OD practitioners are primarily responsible for changing existing patterns to obtain more effective performance and outcomes. While training may be in their bag of tricks, the OD practitioner knows that training is not the solution for every problem. Since the beginning of OD, the practice has had a strong emphasis on groups of individuals or teams as the main conduit for change within an organization. A survey administered to OD practitioners supports this notion. The study found that change management in the form of team development and team building encompassed over one-third of the OD practitioner's time (Waclawski and Church, 2001).

Like other professions, OD practitioners have competencies. And while there are several variations of the competencies needed, we have selected a set of six that were derived from a research study conducted by the University of Michigan Ross School of Business and the RBI Group to share. In this study, data were collected from HR executives representing more than 400 organizations. While they are labeled HR competencies, these six competencies are more aligned with the OD practitioner and, in a sense the case is made for HR and OD professions to come together. The competencies are comprised of both people skills and business acumen, and are outlined in Table 1-2.

Stakeholders

Many stakeholders are involved in OD as well as measurement and evaluation. A stakeholder is defined as any individual or group interested in or affected by the OD intervention. Below are definitions of various stakeholders that may be involved in the OD process.

Table 1-2. OD Competencies

The Credible Activist: With the focus on forming relationships, the practitioner is well respected, offering input, challenging assumptions, and challenging underlying beliefs when needed.
The Operational Executor: With the focus on systems and processes, the practitioner offers impeccable execution of operations while managing people.
The Business Ally: With the focus on systems and processes, possesses business acumen, and understands how business is organized and how it makes money.
The Talent Manager/Organization Designer: With organizational capabilities, masters both research and practice in talent management and organization design.
The Strategy Architect: With organization capabilities, has understanding of how the organization can succeed; actively influences the strategy to fulfill this vision.
The Culture and Change Steward: With organization capabilities, identifies, communicates, and shapes organization culture; and facilitates change to keep business aligned with the most critical needs.

Clients are those individuals who sponsor or fund the OD project. In organizations, the client is usually representative of senior management, executive team, or C-suite. This person may also be a champion behind the success of the project.

Managers immediately supervise individuals involved or affected by the OD intervention. They can be found at any level of management within the organization. They are often a conduit for providing opportunity to implement intervention and make changes.

OD Recipient Stakeholders are those individuals who make up the team or group affected by the OD intervention. They also may be referred to as organization members, team members, group members, participants, stakeholders, or employees.

The Organization is the unit in which the OD intervention is taking place and being evaluated. Organizations may be private or public, for-profit or not-for-profit, government or non-government, academic, or professional associations.

COMMON PITFALLS OF OD PROJECTS: LESSONS LEARNED

The OD literature is copious with reports of failed interventions (Schultz, 2003; Eddy, D'Abate, Tannenbaum, Givens-Skeaton, & Robinson, 2006; Kahnweiler, 2010). With an estimated investment of $156 billion spent on people development (ASTD, 2012), the question is, *why* do OD efforts fail? This section explores 10 reasons that OD projects fail, either in part or entirely. The "build it, they will come" or "one size fits all" mentality is explored in this context. Lighthearted comparisons are made for each pitfall, and pitfalls turn into lessons learned in each of the 10 reasons for failure; hence, the comment made by the late CEO of Coca Cola, Cuban-born Roberto Goizueta, is relevant as we consider lessons learned: "The moment avoiding failure becomes your motivation, you're down a path of inactivity. You stumble only if you're moving" (Gilbert, 2013).

Pitfall #1: Lack of Business Alignment

This is like building a large shopping mall in a town with a population of eight! Based on our research, the number one reason for lack of business results from OD is that interventions have not been aligned to what's most important. Many OD projects are based on external research (what other companies are implementing), with little consideration of the unique organizational landscape and challenges. The old adage "build it, they will come" needs to be challenged as well as the "one size fits all." The assumption that executive coaching or personality testing will change behavior and affect the business is one that warrants questioning. A clearer path is needed between an investment in the organization and the business impact.

Case in Point

For example, one Midwestern organization developed and launched a large leadership program, which cost more than $2 million in its first year. The team that launched the program was asked to evaluate its impact and ROI. This program had already been launched, and because of the financial investment, the question was raised about its impact on the business, and monetary benefit. There was no setting the stage or up-front planning before the program was implemented. The challenge was in understanding why the program was launched to begin with and what business measures it was intended to influence. The project became a fact-finding mission, as the team sought program sponsors who could fill in the gap on the specific business drivers. Four weeks later, the team realized that the program was not adequately aligned to the business, which left major gaps in the evaluation report.

There must be a connection to the business if there is a desire and need to evaluate at the impact level. The principle is a simple one: If the intervention is designed to drive business results and there is a critical reason to measure at this level, the project needs to be aligned to the business measure from the beginning. This process is accomplished by best practice organizations on a routine basis. It is possible to connect OD to a true business need up front.

Too often, OD interventions are based on popular assessment tools, a particular model, or the competencies used in another organization. That does not mean that these tools are never necessary, but OD solutions should address the needs of the organization, in a way that is clear. The selection of a specific intervention should be made by asking, "What is needed in this particular situation?" Understanding what is most critical to the business and aligning OD resources and projects to what matters most, leads to the first lesson learned:

Lesson Learned #1: Align the intervention to business needs in the beginning of the project.

Pitfall #2: Not Conducting Comprehensive Diagnostics

This is like volunteering for a root canal without a dentist's recommendation! Conducting a diagnosis of an organization's needs is the process where an OD practitioner determines the problems, how well the organization functions, and then selects the right intervention. This process usually involves collecting data, which leads to the decision that there are problems that must be addressed. It is important to approach diagnostics from a comprehensive manner, so the solutions prescribed are not superficial or failing to take in the whole picture. Weisbord's (1978) six-box model in approaching diagnostics is outlined here:

1. **Purpose:** Are the mission and goals of the organization clearly understood? Is there agreement and commitment to the organization's mission and goals among the organization's members?
2. **Structure:** Does the organization structure fit the purpose and strategy?
3. **Relationships:** What is the nature of work relationships? How is conflict handled? Is there a healthy interdependence? Are there extremes such as enmeshment or disengagement?
4. **Rewards:** What is rewarded and what is punished in the organization?
5. **Leadership:** How do the leaders lead? What is their style of leadership? Is there congruence between what is said and what is done?
6. **Helpful mechanisms:** Are mechanisms put into place that help performance toward organization goals?

We fold these critical elements into the ROI Methodology by starting with business needs and then, based on the client's input, asking what behaviors, performance, and learning issues are relevant to the business needs. For example, let's assume that during the diagnostic phase, two findings emerge: a decrease in employee satisfaction and a decrease in productivity. This is where the diagnostic phase moves to making inquiry about what behaviors and learning issues may be contributing to the decreased employee satisfaction and productivity. In this case, we discover that inadequate leadership skills and lack of planning are factors contributing to the decreased satisfaction and productivity. This line of questioning and approach to diagnostics not only help identify the right solution, but also set into motion relevant goals and measures. Two key questions follow: 1) What is the ideal or desired state? 2) What is the current state?

These two questions will help to define the gap that exists. For example, a man by the name of Glenn wants to lose weight. He currently weighs 245 pounds and has confirmed with his doctor that he should weigh 195. His weight problem is further complicated by high blood pressure, for which he has been prescribed medication. His doctor has advised him that by losing weight, his blood pressure is likely to decrease. Glenn now has a quantifiable gap, which he has turned into a measurable goal: to lose 50 pounds to decrease blood pressure, and hopefully eliminate the need for medicine. His next step is to identify in what ways his behavior has led to the weight gain. Glenn decides to see a nutritionist and creates a change plan, identifying what behaviors he will change during the week to meet his goals. In his plan, he incorporates exercise four times a week and eating 1800 calories per day. This is quite a change for Glenn, as he has not been exercising or tracking calories. His plan incorporates rewards along the way. For every 10 pounds lost, Glenn can buy either a book he had wanted to read or can go to see a movie. He wasn't factoring in that every time he went to the movies, upon entering the theater, he was overwhelmed by the waft of buttery popcorn. So, his plan needed modification. And eventually, several modifications later, Glenn reached his two goals: 50 pounds of weight loss and stabilized blood pressure. Without collecting the right data (how much weight loss was required), careful planning (deciding on a daily calorie intake and exercise routine), and modifications (changing the rewards), Glenn would not have been on track for a successful change. This leads us to our second lesson learned:

Lesson Learned #2: Conduct thorough organization diagnostics.

Pitfall #3: Not Setting the Stage for Change Management

This is like a dad surprising the family with a newly adopted baby hippo! Change is difficult. Unless there is sense of urgency to change, initiatives move to the back burner. Kotter, in his article "Leading Change: Why Transformations Efforts Fail" (1998), identifies this reason at the top of the list when it comes to understanding why OD initiatives fail. We can confirm that this has been our experience. In his book *Sense of Urgency* (2008), Kotter clarifies that frantic behavior is not the same thing as urgency. This type of approach eventually kills true urgency. True urgency is not fear-based; rather, it is passionately determined to bring about change. Assessment and data are useful tools to create expectation for real change and positive results.

IT projects have a reputation for yeilding mixed results. With over 60 percent of IT projects failing, some experts believe that the most significant challenge when implementing IT projects is change management (Teoh, 2010). Not considering the change factor, resistance to change, and people's attitudes can bring a project to a screeching halt. Fundamentally, IT projects fail because they do not articulate the changes that will occur in the business and therefore fail to prepare an organization for delivery. "It's rare that in implementing a project that the technology does not work; invariably the failure comes from lack of a definition of the way the new business process will work or the fact that people have not been trained to work in a different way. It's change management" (Teoh, 2010). Maybe this is why 79 percent of CEOs responding to a PriceWaterhouseCoopers survey indicated they intend to increase investment on how to manage people through change. For this reason, we listed our third lesson learned as follows:

Lesson Learned #3: Set the stage for change management.

Case in Point

The Government Executive documents a case in point illustrating the need for understanding organization culture. Harmon Davidson, Director of Headquarters Management at Department of Technical Services (DTS), was tasked with conducting a six-month comprehensive survey of headquarter management structure and processes. The results were to be given to the White House as the basis for management reform. Davidson inherited a team from his predecessor. The team was led by Al Pitcher, and comprised of five individuals. Mr. Pitcher's perception of DTS was that their management practices were outdated. To DTS, he came across as "the expert" and seemed uninterested in their history or culture. One week into the survey launch, Davidson received heavy criticism. One staff member in particular voiced her opinion: "Your folks have managed to upset my whole supervisory staff with comments about how we'll have to change our organization and methods. I thought you were going through a fact-finding study. This guy Pitcher sounds like he wants to remake DTS headquarters overnight. Who does he think he is?" This case raises the question of whether DTS headquarters had been properly prepared for the survey, if they understood the context in which it was being administered, and if the survey team understood the organization (Hornesday, 1998).

Pitfall #4: Not Understanding Organization Culture

This is like a North American female wearing a miniskirt in Saudi Arabia! It is estimated that approximately 75 percent of mergers and acquisitions fail because too little effort is focused on culture during integration. Differences in corporate culture have been identified as the major cause for failure to meet shareholder expectations.

Case in Point

For example, in 2005, Sprint and Nextel merged. On paper, the relationship looked like a good fit. Sprint specialized in personal cell phones, long distance, and local phone connections, while Nextel had business infrastructure selling its press-to-talk feature to its loyal customer base from taxi companies, construction crews, and like businesses. The deal went down for a whopping $35 billion, but problems started immediately, such as facing competitors AT&T and Verizon, as well as technology problems. In fact, in almost every aspect of business, they clashed. Nextel employees were accustomed to having a great deal of latitude in offering perks to keep customers loyal, operating in a more entrepreneurial environment. On the other hand, Sprint played customer service by the book, functioning in a more bureaucratic atmosphere. The result was a work environment with declining morale, customer loss, and high turnover. Soon after, Nextel executives began to leave the newly blended family, reporting the two cultures did not mesh well together. Sprint/Nextel started laying off personnel while its stock took a nosedive. It has been described as the "deal from hell" in the *Wall Street Journal* (Moore, February, 2008).

There are countless stories of failed mergers pointing to the two companies not playing well together in the same sandbox. The merger between AOL and Time Warner failed so substantially that it is frequently discussed in business schools. Two very different cultures and ways of doing business merged together. One had a very formal work environment, was focused on Wall Street, with a hierarchical organization that slowed down the decision-making process; whereas the other had a younger workforce, a more entrepreneurial work environment, focused on organic growth. There was no synergy and no meeting of the minds. The $360 billion merger eventually ended in dissolution. Organization culture matters. This leads to the fourth lesson learned:

Lesson Learned #4: Factor organization culture in the OD project plan.

Pitfall #5: Failure to Identify Behavior

This is like planning to lose weight without going on a diet or setting goals! While learning objectives are a requirement for most learning initiatives, it is less common to have behavior change and impact objectives (detailing the business consequences of the organizational behavior change). Writing clear, precise objectives, particularly for behavior and impact levels, is foundational for measurement and evaluation.

Case in Point

A not-for-profit organization anticipated a large segment of their leadership, being Baby Boomers, to retire. The OD group set out to work with the senior leadership team to identify the next generation of leaders. They identified seven leadership behaviors that contributed most to job performance and the organization's strategic objectives. With the behavior change and impact objectives as their guide, the OD group began developing a leadership development program for the next generation of leaders.

Unfortunately, OD practitioners do not always write clear and measurable objectives. The progress made is often delivered by clients asking for the value of the organization development. The good news is that developing objectives can be an easy part of the process. We recommend that at least 50 to 70 percent of OD programs have multilevel objectives, including behavior and impact objectives, although a much smaller number may actually be evaluated at these levels. The fifth lesson learned is simple:

Lesson Learned #5: Establish behavior and impact objectives for OD projects.

Pitfall #6: Not Including the Right People

This is like diluting cough medicine with water and wondering why you still have a cough! OD may have popular initiatives, and several factors cause individuals to want to pursue involvement. If top executives are pushing a particular OD initiative and encouraging participation, there is a tendency for wide-range interest. Some OD interventions, particularly those aimed at executive and leadership development, are often expensive and prominent. Just as students feel proud for being admitted into an honor society, there is a similar pride in being associated with leadership development initiatives. This may cause some individuals who probably do not need to be involved to sign up. Also, when the intended participation group is not well defined, it opens the door for "anyone interested" to attend. This can dilute behavioral and impact outcomes, which affect ROI results. The sixth lesson learned is straightforward:

Lesson Learned #6: Involve the right people at the right time.

Case in Point

The OD group in a Fortune 500 company identified the intended audience for a leadership development program. When the program was launched, the target audience was not consistent and because the company had spent an excess of $1 million on the initiative, they desperately needed attendees to participate. Registration was extended to those who were not leaders but had interest in the subject areas. When the OD group went to measure the effectiveness of the program, the results were negative.

Pitfall #7: Lack of Management Support

Lack of management support is like taking Dad's new car out for a spin without getting permission! Lori Antineau, VP of HR for Talecris Biotherapeutics, said it well: "Once leadership understands that your focus is the same as theirs, it leads to better support to obtain your goals." Lack of management support can impede full implementation of an OD project. While this may not be expected with OD, it is an issue. Imagine if a frontline supervisor participated in a 360-degree assessment and her immediate manager says nothing at all about the assessment. Why was nothing said? Sometimes what is not said is almost as important as what is said. This manager's behavior may undermine the focus of the assessment and the anticipated changes. Warren Bennis (2009) said, "Failing organizations are usually over-managed and under-led." Some would argue that leaders should be more accountable than direct reports, actively engaged and leading, and they should accept the responsibility to reinforce change efforts. This leads to lesson learned number seven:

Lesson Learned #7: Establish supportive partnerships with key managers.

Pitfall #8: Not Building Data Collection Into the Process

Not building data collection into the process is like accepting an online date without first seeing a photo! Perhaps one of the greatest problems with evaluating OD is not being able to secure the appropriate amount and quality of data. The challenge often involves building data collection into the project and positioning data collection as an application tool. In OD, one of the best methods to measure the change and impact, and collect data necessary for the ROI evaluation, is to use an action planning process. This is consistent with OD's foundation of action research. This process provides an opportunity to identify specific actions that will be taken to improve a selected business impact measure. It also allows for processing resistance to change and identifying ways to overcome resistance. Plans are developed during the session and are positioned as application tools to chart the success of implementation. It provides a way to chart changes made and see the results achieved in terms of business impact and even monetary value. The data collection becomes a much easier task when this is properly built in, and participation, completion, and return rates of the action plans can be greatly enhanced. A sample action plan can be seen in chapter 4.

A variety of techniques must be used to secure an appropriate response rate. At least 25 techniques used to improve response rates will be presented in chapter 4. The important point is that data collection needs to be built in to the process, as summarized in the eighth lesson learned:

Lesson Learned #8: Build data collection into the process as a positioned change management tool.

Pitfall #9: Not Isolating the Effects

This is like feeling sick to your stomach and wondering whether it was the pound of cookie dough or the pan of brownies that did it! A key component of the business impact and ROI process is to isolate the effects of the intervention. For example, let us assume that in addition to strategic planning sessions, there are two initiatives: 360-degree assessments and leadership development programs, both occurring simultaneously. Any of these initiatives could contribute to improving the business measures. There are a variety of techniques to isolate the effects including control group comparison, trend-line analysis, and forecasting. These will be described in further detail in chapter 5. The choice of technique will be based on several influences. Whatever the case, it is imperative to build the step of isolation into the process of measuring the effectiveness of OD. The ninth lesson learned is critical to producing a credible study:

Lesson Learned #9: Always isolate the effects of the intervention on impact data.

Pitfall #10: Not Using the Data Routinely for Process Improvement

This is like ignoring the strange smell from the refrigerator! With the ROI Methodology, data are collected along a chain of impact (see Figure 1-1) that must exist for the intervention to add value. If data are collected, adjustments are made. At Levels 1 and 2, when dissatisfaction or learning does not take place as desired, adjustments are made. At Level 3, change indicators may suggest that the team or organization is not making necessary changes. Again, adjustments must be made. At Level 4, business impact, where the business measures are monitored, data are collected to determine what should be adjusted, if necessary. Return on investment is then calculated and the results should be reported to key stakeholders.

FIGURE 1-1. Chain of Impact of an OD Intervention

Stakeholders **react** favorably to the intervention.

Knowledge and skills are **learned**.

New **behavior** is used and **changed**.

The consequences of change are captured as **business impact** measures.

A return on investment is calculated as intervention costs compared with **monetary benefits**.

This reporting is critical to provide recognition, improve processes, show contributions, build support, increase influence, and initiate a variety of other actions needed as data are collected and reported. Collecting data and not using them to drive improvement, or to build credibility and influence, is like planting seeds and not watering them. The result will not be as great.

Any evaluation of OD should be conducted in the spirit of process improvement, not performance evaluation for the team. An entire chapter is devoted to communicating results to the right audience (see chapter 6). The last lesson learned, the 10th, is just as important as the first.

Lesson Learned #10: Use the data collected at different levels to make adjustments and improvements.

Summary of Why OD Projects Fail

Table 1-3 summarizes the 10 reasons for OD project failures.

The lessons learned for organization development have been presented throughout the chapter. The factors are developed from our experience as well as from other research. Not all of the lessons learned need to be addressed. Usually, three to six items are missing for any given project, and these are often critical enough to inhibit the results.

TABLE 1-3. 10 Reasons OD Projects Fail

1.	Lack of business alignment.
2.	Not conducting comprehensive diagnostics.
3.	Not establishing urgency for change.
4.	Organization culture is not understood.
5.	Failure to identify behavior and impact objectives.
6.	Not including the right people.
7.	Lack of management support.
8.	Not building data collection into the process.
9.	Not isolating the effects of the intervention.
10.	Not using the data routinely for process improvement.

To be safe, it is helpful to focus on all of these factors. They represent a solid design for increased accountability, particularly when the impact and ROI are desired. The next chapter discusses the role of organizational culture as it relates to measurement and building a measurement culture.

CURRENT CHALLENGES FOR OD

There are a number of challenges for the field of OD, probably too many to list. We have selected what we believe to be the most significant in this section here:

- Staying in sync with change is one of the biggest challenges. Because the pace of change is at an all-time high, organizations must anticipate and respond to the changing global, technological, and economical demands.
- Building strategic alignment between OD and organization's strategies.
- Having a clear understanding of the needs to drive performance.
- Managing change among worldwide, geographically dispersed populations.
- Obtaining senior leadership understanding and buy-in for OD initiatives.
- Having an overriding guide or plan to address OD needs in a comprehensive and strategic way.
- Misunderstanding from HR and Learning Communities about what OD is and how it functions.
- Perception that OD is too "touchy feely" or ineffective. This was confirmed in a research study by Korten, et al. (2010) that concluded: *OD should discontinue the one-sided emphasis on the soft (social-scientific) side of organizations, and seek a balance with the harder (strategic/business) side.*

- Perception that organization development initiatives are difficult to measure and their outcomes are entirely intangible.
- Lack of evaluation of organization development initiatives that demonstrate impact on the business. Research conducted by Golembiewski and Sun (1990) supported the notion that evaluation of OD was seriously lacking.

Forecast: What's in Store for OD?

Globalization is changing the market and work environments as well as the way organizations function in general. With this large-scale change brings new—and in some cases, even more exaggerated—challenges for OD practitioners. The research field of OD has been changing in the past decade and continues to change in the issues and areas of concerns for OD practitioners. More research is needed in many areas, but particularly in the area of applying the OD practice to international or cross-cultural settings, as well as implementing systematic ways to measure the effectiveness of OD. We don't have a crystal ball, but our forecast is based on research, understanding general needs of organizations today, and patterns we have observed in the context of OD:

- In the PricewaterhouseCoopers survey, 68 percent of CEOs said they intend to increase investment in leadership and talent development as a result of the global recession, suggesting that existing practices did not support businesses when the global recession hit. This is prime information for OD.
- Globalization has brought about a more global workplace and diverse workforce, causing OD efforts to be effective in cross-cultural settings. OD practitioners will need the necessary international/cross-cultural competence to work with an increasingly diverse and international workforce.
- Information technology (IT) is redefining how work is done, bringing about a new business model altogether. Today, organizations collect, store, and transmit data in ways that increase productivity and lower costs in innovative ways. According to Marketing Forecasts (2011), e-commerce is projected to grow in double digits. IT has allowed for organizations to increase the knowledge base as well as reduce the workforce. This has a tremendous impact on the field of OD, not only in accelerating learning to the changing needs of business and e-commerce, but also in being a conduit for change for rapidly changing work environments. This has relevant implications for OD practitioners in assisting with organization design and structure, business processes, and managing change.
- Projected growth in e-commerce also has implications for the OD practitioner to match its delivery mode of interventions with the use of technology itself. This growth forces us to raise the bar for OD and its use of technology to help support and deliver OD initiatives. Of course, a benefit of using technology in OD work is

that it will reduce the time it takes to effectively complete the effort. In addition, the role of social media is becoming a viable avenue for OD practitioners to network, promote, and market their business. OD practitioners will likely increase their use of social media in their businesses in the coming years.

- The need for demonstrating alignment to strategy and outcomes of OD efforts is evident. OD has reached a critical juncture in showing how it aligns with what's important for the organization and in showing meaningful outcomes that measure results. This is not expected to decrease—just the opposite. More and more, we should expect to show alignment with the business.
- There will always be a special place in the OD field for innovation. One of the strengths OD brings to the table is helping to identify creative solutions to old problems. In the past decade, innovation has increased in OD practitioners offering services, demonstrating that the trend will continue in the future.

FINAL THOUGHTS

This chapter set the stage for the book by defining key OD terms and relevant examples of OD practice to make these definitions practical. These terms are followed by lessons learned for OD project implementation. Finally, challenges in the field of OD are explored while a forecast of what's in store for OD are identified.

Developing a Measurement Culture

Try to see your culture as a positive force to be used rather than a constraint to be overcome.

—Edgar Schein

Many organizations are recognizing the importance of culture, once perceived to be vague, now as an everyday practice in organizations today. "The Rise of the Chief Culture Officer," an article in the July 2012 edition of *Fortune* magazine, discusses the position of Chief Culture Officer (CCO), which is held at a number of progressive organizations. The CCO's prime duty: to focus on maintaining core parts of culture that contribute to the organization's success.

Google has a CCO who ensures certain aspects valued by the organization are kept. Its work environment is known for being unconventional; Google's employees have access to rock climbing walls and foreign language classes. Some employees boast they go to work in their pajamas, play foosball, and glide around the building on Razor scooters. An organization that places value on creativity and innovation, Google has bathroom stalls with high-tech commodes and a quiz on the inside of each door called *Testing the Toilet*, presenting brainy challenges for software engineers.

Google is also described as being a measurement-driven organization. By defining objectives up front, the organization sets out to collect the right data and then, allow the data to drive the decision-making process. For example, in the people analytics department, they collected data to answer the question as to whether managers matter. Using regression analysis, the team was able to show that a certain type of manager had better performing teams with happier employees. Once they defined this type of manager they were able to measure their managers against a specific type of criteria, and revise their management training (Marr, 2012).

While organization culture is increasingly observed as a critical factor in success, the implications of measurement in organization culture are also significant. This chapter explores the role of culture in measurement. To build a culture of measurement, certain steps need to be taken, and it is in this context that the ROI Methodology is presented. In this chapter, we address using the ROI Methodology with OD interventions and how OD practitioners are conduits of change in building a measurement culture.

LEADERSHIP AND CULTURE

Leadership is at the core of organization culture. It is impossible to understand organization culture without understanding leadership and its role to form and reinforce cultural norms and values. Leaders set a precedence of what's important (Schein, 1992). Even though founders and CEOs also give form and establish an organization's behavior, cultures have been known to change in the hands of succeeding leaders (Kerr and Shocum, 2005). What gets rewarded, what kinds of things are given importance, what values rise to the top, and what kinds of things are frowned upon or discouraged. Leadership and culture go hand-in-hand.

What leaders systematically and routinely pay attention to speaks volumes. This often comes in the form of measures and reports. When leaders review operational reports and success toward measures, it sets forth a powerful motion for the organization to align itself toward behaving and acting toward improving outcomes. When leaders are inconsistent or do not convey clarity on what needs to be measured, employees are left with confusion around what needs to be done and how to proceed.

The body of literature on leadership and organization culture is growing. Jim Collins (2001), in his landmark research culminating in *Good to Great*, identifies a particular style of leadership as characteristic of organizations categorized as "great." The style of leadership he observed, named *Level 5 Leadership*, involves a paradoxical blend of personal humility and internal strength or ambition. Ego needs were checked at the door. In these cases, the leader was not interested in receiving recognition or credit; rather, she was interested in a job of excellence. These leaders cared about the long-term endurance of the organization, sometimes leaving someone behind who was equal to the task so the organization would continue to be a success. Collins also noted that the great companies had values of individual freedom and responsibility, empowering employees to do whatever it takes to get the job done. This, of course, was communicated and reinforced by leadership. Collins's research, along with others, points to the need for defining characteristics and values of high-performing cultures.

HIGH-PERFORMING CULTURE

High-performing cultures have been associated with strong financial outcomes; however, these cultures also have strong employee motivation and performance. Research has shown specific cultural characteristics directly related to organization effectiveness and outcomes (Quinn and Spreitzer, 1991; Cameron and Freeman, 1991; Denison and Mishra, 1993). High-performance organizations tend to have cultures that share five common traits:

1. **Empowering Style Leadership:** Leaders communicate with respect and lead by example. Employees are empowered to use their judgment to make

decisions and take action in their day-to-day jobs. Employees are not present to serve management or reinforce bureaucracy. Leadership is supportive of employees, with focus on helping to support employees so they can be freed up to focus on caring for customers.

2. **Collaborative Environment:** This type of environment is inclusive; employees have a sense of belonging, with everyone sharing the responsibilities of identifying problems and coming up with solutions. These types of organizations are highly participatory.
3. **Strong Core Values:** Values of respect, loyalty, and integrity are embedded in leadership behaviors toward employees, and permeates throughout the organization.
4. **Planning:** Employees know what the long-term plans are for the company and how to get there. Strategy is well-defined and priorities are also clear. Plans are clearly articulated and there are specific measures to assess the success of the plans. Employees know what is important for the organization and what requires attention to do their jobs effectively.
5. **Measurement and Feedback:** High-performing organizations not only plan and prioritize what is most important for the business, but they also set into motion indicators and measures to know whether they are hitting the mark or not. Terminology such as "data-driven organizations" is also used to describe this environment. Employees also receive ongoing feedback so performance is collaboratively assessed as it relates to the business.

Core to applying strategy is understanding organization culture and how to uniquely implement strategic initiatives to achieve successful outcomes. Table 2-1 shows descriptions of leadership styles in understanding organization culture.

What does organization culture have to do with effectiveness and measurement? This next section shows the relationship between organization culture and effectiveness. Chapter 8 has a case study of organization culture change with the use of the ROI Methodology. Later in this chapter, we will build upon organization culture by looking at building a measurement culture and then ultimately, showing how the ROI Methodology is used with organization culture interventions.

Organization Culture and Effectiveness

The relationship between organization culture and effectiveness has been established through various research studies. Group culture was the subject for subsequent research that examined group culture among academic institutions. Those universities scoring higher on group culture items also had higher scores on student satisfaction ratings as well as faculty and staff satisfaction (Cameron and Freeman, 1991).

TABLE 2-1. Organization Culture Descriptions

Autocratic	Democratic	Closely Supervised	Empowered
Tightly controls employees; hierarchical, dominating leadership	Inclusive; values participation and gathering input from employees	Employees need to constantly check in for permission; leaders tightly manage employees, down to minutiae/details	Promotes employees' independence; entrust responsibility and authority to complete tasks

Other studies have demonstrated positive relationships between organization culture and organization effectiveness. Stock, et al. (2006) found a positive relationship between organization cultural characteristics and error reduction outcomes. In his study, he found that the more an organization was collaborative and operated as a cohesive group, the higher the impact on error reduction. GTE also conducted a workplace study that found those leaders who had an empowering style of leadership also had significantly lower billing inaccuracies when compared to leaders who maintained more control.

The implication of these studies is that there are organizational cultural characteristics that play a pivotal role in organization effectiveness. Measurement and feedback is one of the components described as a feature of a high-performing culture. In this next section, we describe the benefits and aspects of building a measurement culture.

While there are many advantages for operating in a measurement culture, we have highlighted a few of the ones ranking at the top of the list:

1. **Measurement cultures lay the foundation for organization learning.** Information sharing is leveraged in the organization toward knowledge and growth.
2. **Measurement cultures provide the way for projects and departments to track their progress.** This allows for managers to track progress toward department goals. Managers need to know the score; and tracking the progress at specific times will help to define progress. What happens if the project that is implemented is a flop? Or if needs are not fully met? Tracking along the way allows for managers and team members to make modifications if needed so that outcomes move in a favorable direction.
3. **Measurement cultures make data-driven decisions.** The use of the "hunch" takes second place to making decisions based on data, inevitably leading organizations to drive sound decision making. If a project is not going in the direction it needs to go, then the data will validate this point. And when collecting the right data, it should help pinpoint where things broke down.

HOW AND WHY OD FITS WITH ROI

Motives and behaviors of OD practitioners is a topic of great interest for today's OD professional. OD practitioners tend to be more socially driven (to help others) rather than financially driven (Church, Hurley, and Burke, 1992; Margulies and Raia, 1990). So what would drive an OD practitioner to pursue ROI? Perhaps this is best answered by considering how and why ROI will help the OD process and ultimately, help the client by showing both tangible and intangible ways that the intervention has yielded the desired change. Three case studies are included in this book in chapters 8, 9, and 10, which show application of the ROI Methodology to OD.

The OD Practitioner as a Change Agent

Practitioners in the field of OD often view their role as one who influences an individual, group, or organization toward desired change. The change agent plays a significant role in leading the change effort or collaborating with the team assigned to initiating change. Trying to create an environment that is measurement friendly also involves a change agent—someone to lead this effort and manage the change process within an organization. Several key aspects include:

- Building a measurement culture should be a strategic change. Set the stage with the "why" behind building a measurement culture. This change effort needs to be in sync with what's important for the organization.
- Involve someone who is senior in the organization, someone who has clout to pave the way for building a measurement culture.
- Include action planning and feedback to keep momentum in building a measurement culture.

Identify a System to Routinely Review Measures

Adopting a systematic way to plan, collect, analyze, and report on initiatives in the organization sets in motion the process of communicating and reinforcing what is important to the organization. This also sends a clear message to key stakeholders as to what areas of change need to take place to improve outcomes. This is particularly true when measurement has been planned in advance to collect data points that will tell the story in a comprehensive way.

The ROI Methodology is a proven approach to plan, collect, analyze, and communicate outcomes that measure organization development initiatives. Later in this chapter, we address the fit, logic, and business case for using the ROI Methodology in measuring organization development.

In Table 2-2, there is a clear delineation between activity-based and results-based initiatives. The old "build it, they will come" mentality is challenged through a series of filtering questions.

- Is this initiative aligned with business impact or organization effectiveness outcomes?
- Is there an assessment of performance that shows a gap in performance? Is the work environment prepared to reinforce the implementation of the OD initiative?
- Have partnerships been established with key stakeholders to support this initiative?
- Are there specific measurable objectives for expected behavior change and business impact?

The more OD initiatives are aligned with results-based initiatives, or what's important to the organization, the more likely OD initiatives can be easily measured. The more OD initiatives can help to establish measures for employee performance, the more likely there will be impact to the organization in terms of effectiveness. The old adage rings true in this context: *What gets measured gets done* (Tom Peters, 1986).

OD AND THE ROI METHODOLOGY

The role of measurement and evaluation is crucial for establishing the impact and credibility of OD as a field. It is time for the field to fully accept its roots in a data-driven approach and understand the value inherent in measuring how and what we do.

This section presents the reasons for using the ROI Methodology to measure the effectiveness of organization development. To build the business case for using the ROI Methodology, we will explore its essential components, describe the types of OD effectiveness data that support the use of the ROI Methodology, and share an example of how ROI is a viable tool for measuring the effectiveness of organization development.

Of particular interest to the topic of this book is the relationship between organization culture and characteristics and return on investment. Waclawski and Church (2001) observed this need, nothing that proven methods leading to financial as well as humanistic gains were a requirement for OD. Denison (1990) also explored the relationship between OD and ROI by showing that higher group decision-making ratings were positively correlated to higher return on investment.

Table 2-2. Activity-Based vs. Results-Based Approach to Organizational Development

Activity-Based	Results-Based
Business need is not linked to the organizational development initiative in terms of monetary impact.	Initiative is linked to specific business impact or organizational effectiveness measures such as customer satisfaction, productivity, employee satisfaction, and so on.
Assessment of performance issues that will be addressed in organizational development initiative are not captured in a quantifiable, measurable manner.	A quantifiable gap assessment of performance effectiveness has been identified.
Specific measurable, quantifiable objectives are not clarified.	Specific, measurable objectives for behavior change and the related business impact are identified.
Employees are not fully engaged or prepared to participate in the project/initiative.	Results expectations are communicated with and in partnership with employees.
The environment is not prepared to reinforce the application/implementation of the OD initiative to ensure behavior change and business impact.	Work environment is prepared to reinforce the application/implementation of the OD initiative to ensure behavior change and business impact.
Partnerships with key stakeholders to support the implementation have not been identified and developed.	Partnerships are established with key stakeholders prior to implementation to ensure participation and support.
Results or benefit-cost analysis in real, tangible, and objective measures—including monetary impact—are not captured.	Results and benefit-cost analysis are measured.
Planning and reporting is input-focused.	Planning and reporting is outcome-focused.

A Rationale for Return on Investment

Several features about return on investment make it an effective measure for organization development:

- **To show bottom-line results for OD interventions.** In the range of measurement possibilities, return on investment represents the ultimate—a comparison of the actual cost of a project to its monetary benefits. This is done by using the same standard ratio that accountants have used for years to show the return on investment for a variety of investments, such as technology, equipment. and buildings.
- **Return on investment has a rich history of application.** The ROI Methodology is not a passing trend used in today's organizations. It is a measure

of accountability that has been in place for centuries. When resources are invested to address a business need, the ROI Methodology shows the financial impact of the investment.

- **To speak the same language of senior management.** Most managers in an organization have knowledge and skills on how to manage the business. Some have university degrees or even master's degrees in business administration. These managers understand the need for a process to establish a solid business case and to calculate a return on investment. They use ROI for a variety of projects and are fluid in carrying on conversations that measure the monetary results from large investments.
- **Return on investment generates a high degree of attention among key stakeholders.** The positive ROI outcomes create buzz and attention, particularly when the ROI value exceeds expectations. Most stakeholders involved in organization development projects intuitively believe that the interventions add value. Return on investment, as a measurement tool, confirms this hunch using a credible and valid process.
- **The use of ROI Methodology forces the issue of strategic alignment.** By following the steps in the ROI process—conducting diagnostics with a multi-level framework for understanding business and performance needs—OD interventions will be more closely aligned with strategic and operational needs of the business.

Gone are the days of indiscriminately increasing human capital investments with no evidence as to their impact on the business. In times of budget cuts, human capital rises to the top of consideration and organization development projects are no exception.

These five factors are foundational for executives and OD practitioners to rethink the use of ROI Methodology and to implement this type of evaluation in specific projects. Through the use of ROI Methodology, stakeholder groups receive a comprehensive set of significant and balanced information about the success of an organization development intervention.

Types of Data for the ROI Methodology

At the heart of the ROI Methodology is the variety of data collected throughout the process and reported at different intervals. Some of the data are assigned a level because they reflect a successive effect in which one type of data affects the next.

The concept of levels is an old one. There are very logical steps of succession in numerous tasks and fields. Their use in a sequence can be linked to a variety of guidelines and models. For example, Bloom uses levels to describe his taxonomy of learning. Bloom makes a distinction between comprehension and application in the context of learning. The medical field also uses levels to run and analyze blood work. This helps in not only the clinician understanding the categories represented by the levels but also helps the patient understand his results. The ROI Methodology is based on levels of evaluation, as shown in Figure 2-1.

The good news is that the ROI Methodology works extremely well in all types of environments and projects, particularly in organization development. An initiative would likely be unsuccessful if an adverse reaction occurred, so the first level is critical. Also, an element of learning is required to make an initiative successful. Regardless of the type of initiative involved, those participating usually acquire knowledge and skills. Of course, some projects require significant skill development. However, learning does not guarantee success. Follow-up is needed to ensure knowledge and skills are used appropriately; therefore, application and implementation are critical for effectiveness; failure in these areas is typically what causes project failure overall. This is consistent with Lewin's refreezing phase. Sustaining implementation is key. In chapter 7, we go into more depth on sustaining the effects of the OD intervention with the tools of measurement and evaluation.

The most important data set for those who sponsor projects is the impact—the consequence of application—often expressed in business terms as output, quality, costs, and time. For some executives, showing the impact of an intervention isn't enough. They want to know something else, which pushes evaluation to the ultimate level of accountability: return on investment. Return on investment is the amount of improvement at the impact level (attributed to the program), converted to money and compared to the cost of the program.

Figure 2-1 describes six categories of data that can be used to measure the comprehensive outcomes of OD interventions. As the evaluation moves to the higher levels, the value ascribed to the data by the client increases. However, the degree of effort and cost of capturing the data for the higher levels of evaluation generally increase as well. With proper project planning and preparation, costs can be minimized. The following sections describe the various qualitative and quantitative measures listed in Figure 2-1, which are essential to the ROI Methodology.

Project Cost Data

Level 0, Inputs and Indicators, represents a category of data that reveals the cost of an OD project. It reflects all direct costs (such as software) and indirect costs (such as client time in the project). Level 0 data do not represent outcome data, but they are important data as they represent the investment in OD.

Reaction Data

The first category of outcome data collected from a project is basic reaction data (Level 1 evaluation). This type of data represents an immediate reaction to the intervention from a variety of key stakeholders, particularly those charged with the responsibility to make it work. At this level, a variety of basic satisfaction and reaction measures are taken, often representing five to 15 separate measures to gain insight into the value, importance, relevance, and usefulness of the intervention.

Learning Data

As the project continues, new information is acquired and new skills are learned. This category of outcome data (Level 2) focuses on the changes in knowledge and skill acquisition and details what needs to be learned. Some solutions have a high learning component, such as those involved in a comprehensive, long-term leadership development program. Others may have a low learning component, such as a brief team-building session. In some cases, the focus is on organization learning or departmental skill development. In short, the focus of this level is learning.

Behavior Change and Implementation Data

Behavior change and implementation are key measures that show the extent to which behavior is changed or performance is improved (Level 3). This type of data reflects outcomes associated with actions taken, adjustments made, new skills applied, habits changed, and steps in a new process initiated as a result of the OD intervention. Given that change management is key for OD interventions, measures of organization change or subsystems' measures of change would be observed in this level of data.

This is one of the most powerful categories of data because it uncovers not only the extent to which the intervention is implemented but also the reasons for lack of success. At this level, barriers and enablers to application and implementation are detailed, and a complete profile of performance change at the various steps of implementation is provided.

Business Impact Data

Behavior change or actions taken have consequences. These consequences can be described in one or more measures representing an impact on the work environment, an impact directly on a given team department, or an impact on other parts of the organization. Organization effectiveness measures are generally categorized in this level of data.

This level of data (Level 4) reflects the specific business impact and may include measures such as output, quality, costs, time, job satisfaction, and customer satisfaction that have been influenced by the application of the OD project. A direct link

FIGURE 2-1. Six Categories of Data

Level	Measurement Focus	Typical Measures
0–Inputs and Indicators ⬇	• Inputs into the initiatives including indicators representing scope, volumes, costs, and efficiencies	• Types of topics, content. • Number of initiatives • Number of people • Hours of involvement • Costs
1–Reaction, Satisfaction, and Planned Action ⬇	• Reaction to the initiative including the perceived value of the project	• Relevance • Importance • Usefulness • Appropriateness • Intent to use • Motivational
2–Learning and Confidence ⬇	• Knowledge gained, learning how to use the content and materials, including the confidence to use what was learned	• Skills • Learning • Knowledge • Capacity • Competencies • Confidences • Contacts
3–Behavior Change, Performance, and Implementation ⬇	• Behavior change, change in performance, use of content and materials in the work environment, including progress with implementation	• Behavior change • Extent of use • Task completion • Frequency of use • Actions completed • Success with use • Barriers to use • Enablers to use
4–Impact and Effectiveness ⬇	• The impact of the use of the content and materials expressed as business impact and effectiveness measures	• Productivity • Revenue • Quality • Time • Efficiency • Customer Satisfaction • Employee Engagement
5–ROI	• Comparison of monetary benefits from the intervention to intevention costs	• Benefit-cost ratio (BCR) • ROI (%) • Payback period

between business impact and the project must be established for the project to drive business value. At this level of analysis, a technique must be used to isolate the effects of the project from other influences that may be driving the same measure. Answering the following question is imperative: "How do you know it was the organization development intervention that caused the improvement and not something else?"

Return on Investment Data

This level of data compares the monetary value of the business impact measures to the actual cost of the project. It is the ultimate level of accountability and represents the financial impact directly linked with the intervention, expressed as a benefit-cost ratio (BCR) or return on investment percentage. This measure is the fifth level of evaluation (Level 5). It requires converting business impact data to monetary value and comparing that value to the fully-loaded cost of the OD project.

Intangible Data

Intangible data consist of measures that are not converted to monetary value. In some cases, however, converting certain measures to monetary values is not credible with a reasonable amount of resources. In these situations, data are listed as an intangible, but only if they are linked to the OD intervention.

Satisfaction leads to learning, which leads to behavior change, which leads to business impact, and ultimately to return on investment. At the business impact level, the effects of the intervention must be isolated from other influences. Also, business impact data are converted to monetary value and compared to the cost of the intervention to develop the return on investment. Stakeholders will more readily understand this chain of impact as they consider the long-term success of OD initiatives. It is a novel yet pragmatic way to show the results of OD interventions.

ROI Process Model

Measurement and evaluation must be systematic, following a standard process that can be duplicated to a variety of projects. The ROI Process Model is a 10-step process, illustrated in Figure 2-2 (on the following page). The process begins with the end in mind, by creating objectives and proceeds through until an impact report is generated. The model is highly adaptable to the needs of the project in question, as the evaluation can stop at any point along the process. The data collected during the intervention at Level 1 and Level 2, and data collected after the intervention at Levels 3 and 4 are steps along the way. This process will be explained in further detail in chapter 3.

FIGURE 2-2. ROI Methodology Process Model

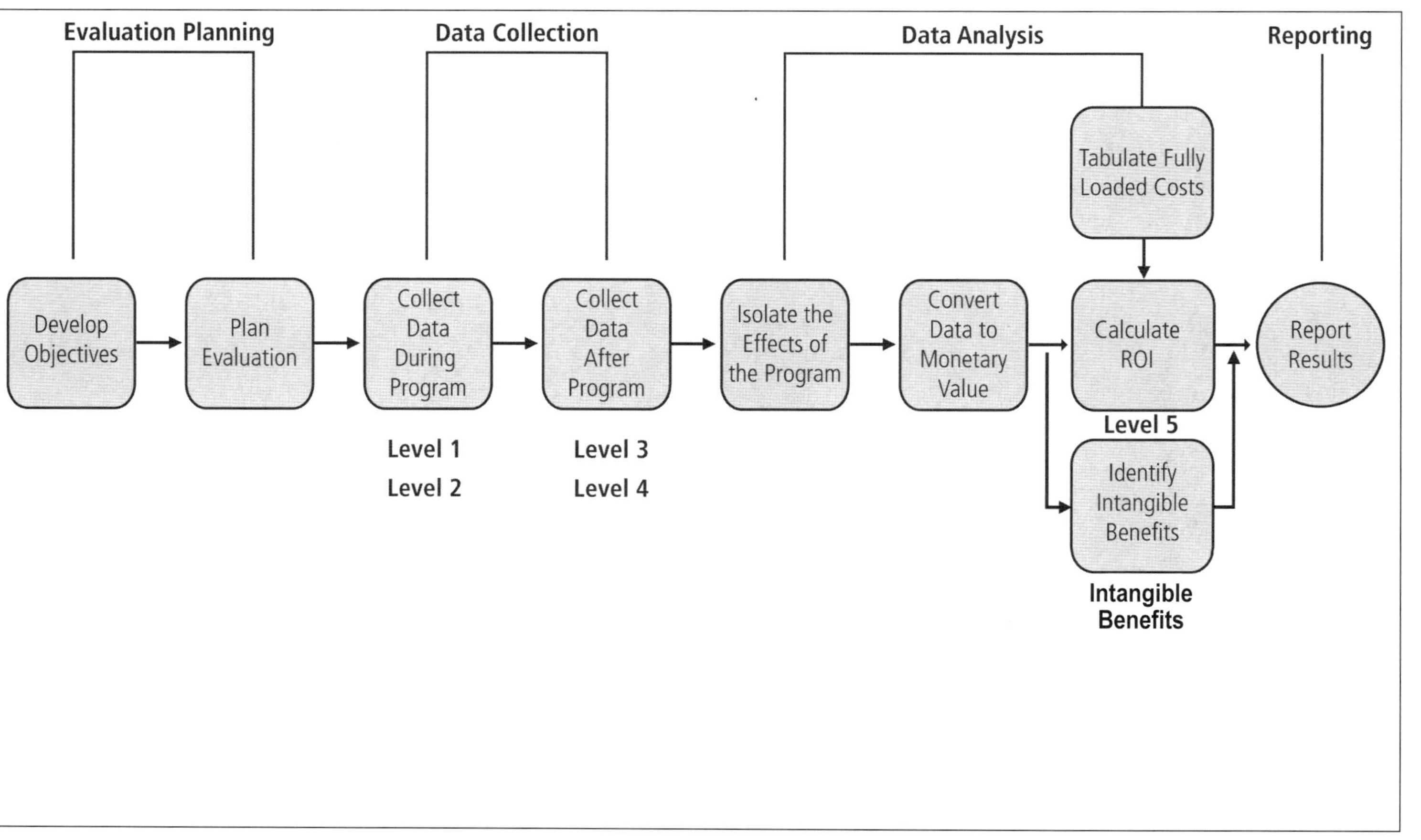

Source: ©ROI Institute.

FINAL THOUGHTS

This chapter has provided not only an explanation of organization culture but also presented why it is so important in the context of the OD practice. Building on the premise that organization culture matters, this chapter explores ways for OD practitioners to be change agents and build a measurement culture within the organizations where they work. Finally, an introduction to the ROI Methodology is provided as a process to use in building measurement cultures.

3

Alignment and Evaluation Planning

It pays to plan ahead. It wasn't raining when Noah built the ark.
—Richie Frost

An external consultant specializing in OD was asked to join a small internal OD team working on a leadership initiative for a large banking organization. In particular, the OD team wanted the consultant to help with evaluating the leadership program. By the time the consultant was invited to assist the team, the leadership program had already been launched and there were no measures put into place. There were missed opportunities to gather reaction and learning data as the program had commenced. To identify relevant measures, the consultant began to ask questions about the why behind the intervention; the team members indicated they were unsure and that their project sponsor had left the organization. Not only was the external consultant called after the fact, or after the program had launched, but now was presented with the challenge of no identifiable performance or business measures. After confirming that needs assessment did take place, the consultant set out to inquire from others in the organization who could help to supply missing information from the needs assessment. Weeks passed and finally, the consultant was able to confirm several significant performance and business needs that tied into the program, including leadership skills, conducting performance appraisals, giving and receiving feedback, turnover, employee satisfaction, and productivity.

The issues raised by this scenario represent challenges and experiences common to those practicing evaluation—pursuing initiatives without knowing why and not identifying clear performance or business needs or measures up front. Evaluation is too often considered an afterthought, as illustrated by this case. This chapter explores why it is important to plan ahead, how to select interventions for ROI analysis, how to align OD projects with business needs using the V-Model, the process of integrating OD diagnostics with the ROI Methodology, and the steps and artifacts included in evaluation planning.

SELECTING INTERVENTIONS FOR ROI ANALYSIS

Every OD initiative should be evaluated in some way, even if that involves only satisfaction data collected from those involved in the intervention. While reaction data alone may be sufficient for evaluating some OD interventions, the challenge is to collect additional data at higher levels, and to do so when it is relevant and feasible.

Appropriate evaluation is usually determined when the intervention is initiated, recognizing that the evaluation level may change throughout the life of the intervention. For example, the UN raises awareness on gender equality. The objective is to increase awareness and advocacy for women. The awareness factors can be evaluated with reaction (Level 1) and learning (Level 2) data, ensuring that awareness and learning take place. Later, a follow-up may be implemented to determine whether the information provided in the intervention and actions are taken toward advocacy for women. This follow-up is an example of behavior change/performance evaluation (Level 3).

If the cost of this intervention increases, sponsors may ask to evaluate the impact (Level 4) and even ROI (Level 5) of the intervention. The important point is that during the life of a particular intervention, the desired level of evaluation may change. Because of the resources required and the realistic barriers for ROI implementation, ROI analysis is used only for particular interventions that meet several criteria, as outlined in the following pages.

Recommended Interventions for Evaluation at Lower Levels

Reaction evaluation can suffice as the only level of evaluation for short interventions, such as briefings, policy introductions, and general information that is distributed. If reaction to the intervention is critical, ongoing assessment of reaction may be necessary. For example, an ethics briefing is measured at Level 1, capturing the extent to which employees perceive the intervention as fair, appropriate, and helpful.

Learning evaluation (Level 2) is suitable when learning, knowledge, or skills are needed. With most OD interventions, learning evaluation is important. For example, in implementing a new business process, it is helpful to know whether the team members are able to demonstrate they can use the steps in the process.

Behavior change and performance evaluation (Level 3) is necessary when the target audience must perform or behave in a particular way as a result of the intervention. For example, most team leaders are required to use team leadership skills in directing their teams' use of new processes. Evaluation at Level 3 may be necessary to measure success. Observations may be used to ensure that they are using desired behavior with their teams. Other methods are also available to evaluate key interventions at Level 3, depending on the needs and culture of the organization.

Deciding which type of evaluation is sometimes a trade-off with resources available and the amount of disruption allowed collecting data. Because some data collection at this level may disrupt work at varying degrees or inconvenience those involved in some way, the evaluation needs to be balanced with the time, effort, and resources that can be committed to the process. Many organizations fall short of the ideal evaluation and settle for a feasible approach within existing constraints.

Recommended Interventions for Impact and Return on Investment Analysis

Interventions taken to the levels of business impact and ROI analysis meet certain criteria; it's important to understand the contributions they make to the organization. The criteria for selecting interventions to evaluate with business impact and ROI data are outlined below.

Expected Duration of the Intervention

The first criterion is the duration of the intervention. Some interventions are brief, designed to react to a particular aspect on a team, and ROI analysis may not be necessary. Facilitating a one-hour Myers-Briggs Type Indicator session with an intact work team is an example of a short cycle intervention. ROI evaluation at this level may not be necessary. On the other hand, some interventions have a longer life cycle, such as an organization culture change project. Consequently, at some point in the life cycle of this intervention, conducting a comprehensive analysis may be helpful.

Linkage to Strategic Initiatives

Strategic initiatives are those designed to address specific strategic objectives. These strategic initiatives are so important that they should be subjected to a high level of scrutiny. For example, a chain of hospitals implemented an intervention to support a strategic goal that would transform the way patients were cared for and treated. The intervention was a multi-year change and became a candidate for ROI analysis because it was linked to this strategic initiative.

Cost of the Intervention

High cost interventions need to be evaluated in a comprehensive manner to ensure they are adding value. The higher the cost, the greater the need for ROI analysis. For example, a U.S.-based technology firm implemented an expensive OD intervention costing $1.7 million, warranting ROI analysis.

Time Commitment

Interventions that involve large amounts of time are also suitable candidates for business impact and ROI analysis. This is different than the criterion of duration of the program, because it's about the segments of time that participants are sacrificing to participate. If significant time is taken from their jobs to support the intervention, this is a good reason for pursuing the higher level of analysis. For example, executives from a pharmaceutical company questioned the value of a 360-degree feedback process because it required so much of the managers' time. The time involved ultimately led to an ROI study.

Visibility of the Intervention

Highly visible interventions lead to the need for accountability at higher levels. For example, a large South African electric utility conducted a two-week intervention, the Organization Challenge, each year for middle-level managers who were destined to be top executives. Extensive publicity made it a high profile initiative; thus, it was important to show the business impact and monetary value of the program.

Management Interest

The extent of management interest is often the most critical issue in driving interventions for impact and ROI analysis. Senior management has concerns about some interventions, but not all of them. Sometimes, management interest may go hand-in-hand with visibility or costs associated with the intervention. For example, executives at a financial company questioned the impact of an OD intervention and how it contributed to improvement measures. This led to an impact study being conducted.

Client Requirement

Particularly since the global recession, sponsors of OD projects ask for their results. Increasingly, executives are concerned about expenditures. For major and significant interventions, they may require an ROI calculation. For example, a major European oil company required an impact study of an executive leadership intervention developed by a prestigious university on the West Coast of the United States. The top executives said, "We must see results from this intervention because it takes a lot of time, commitment, energy, and resources."

Interventions Unsuitable for ROI Analysis

There are factors to consider that help filter out those interventions that are unsuitable for ROI analysis. Interventions that are mandated are often not good candidates for ROI analysis. For example, a series of performance tools such as guides, tips, and notes are made available to a department. These are reinforcing tools that are unlikely to generate a positive return on investment, making evaluation at this level questionable. With limited resources for this level of analysis, the mandated interventions are typically not subject to ROI evaluation unless executives want to pursue it for some reason.

Finally, as noted earlier, interventions of short duration are also inappropriate for impact and ROI analysis. For an intervention to add value, a change in behavior must take place. Brief interventions do not typically drive this type of change. For example, a one-hour virtual module will not usually drive a significant behavior change. This can also be said for interventions with small groups of people.

INTEGRATING DIAGNOSTICS WITH THE ROI METHODOLOGY

The basis for an organization intervention adding value rests on the rationale for its existence and the extent to which it relates to a specific business need. This fundamental concept requires thorough diagnostics, which is foundational to the beginning point in the ROI Methodology. As described in chapter 1, by conducting diagnosis or assessment of the organization's needs, it allows the OD practitioner to determine with the help of the client the necessary interventions. Schein (1987) rightfully advocated for a consultative process approach, avoiding the trap of falling into the doctor-patient role; rather, using a more process-oriented method to intervene on the mutually agreeable goals. This sets the stage for collecting all the necessary data, minimizing defensiveness and resistance.

While there are a variety of methods to approach diagnostics, it is critical to integrate the ROI Methodology when planning to measure at higher levels of evaluation. In chapter 1, we outlined the use of the six-box method with diagnostics (Weisbord, 1982). The elements of Weisbord's model are common to others. Below is a list of the common areas for diagnostics:

- **Purpose:** Is the organization's mission and strategy clear and supported by the organization's members?
- **Structure:** Does the organization's structure fit the purpose and strategy?
- **Relationships:** What is the nature of work relationships? How are communication and conflict handled?
- **Rewards:** What is rewarded and what is punished in the organization?
- **Leadership:** What is the style of leadership? Is it more empowering or more micromanaging? Is there congruence between what is said and what is done?
- **Helpful mechanisms:** Are there systems and tools in place to support performance in the organization?

Making inquiry on these matters sets the stage for the use of the ROI Methodology. For example, let's assume during the diagnostic phase, two findings emerge: high turnover and low productivity. This is where the diagnostic phase moves to making inquiry about what leadership behaviors, rewards, and helpful mechanisms may be contributing to the high turnover and decreased productivity. And in this case, we discover that leadership behavior is causing most of the problems, but the leadership is not aware of how profound the problem is. The solution in this case involves increasing awareness as well as developing leaders to behave in productive ways. Not only does this approach to diagnostics help to identify the right solution, but it sets into motion relevant goals and measures. Two key questions follow: 1) What is the ideal or desired state? 2) What is the current state? These two questions will help to quantify the gap that exists.

ALIGNING OD PROJECTS WITH THE BUSINESS

Most of the existing evaluation models have been developed to enhance, modify, or improve what Don Kirkpatrick initially published 50 years ago (Kirkpatrick, 1998). His basic premise of considering evaluation as steps of measuring reaction, learning, behavior, and results, brought a novel and useful approach to practitioners. In the 1970s, Jack Phillips added a fifth level along with a 10-step process, and included the critical step of isolating the effects of the solution (Phillips 1983; Phillips, 2003). He also included a set of standards to ensure reliable implementation of the process model. The combined Kirkpatrick-Phillips approach probably accounts for 80 to 90 percent of the evaluation models used today worldwide.

Phillips's V-Model is a powerful method to ensure business alignment. As shown in Figure 3-1 the V-Model maps the linkage from the needs assessment for projects to objectives and evaluation. This figure shows the important linkage between the initial problem or opportunity that created the need for the intervention, and its evaluation. It also shows the three points at which business alignment occurs: at the beginning of the project, during the project, and during the follow-up evaluation in order to validate the alignment.

The V-Model is based on the concept of the five levels of evaluation. As we will explore throughout this book, you will see that organization development is a natural candidate for the Phillips ROI Methodology and its alignment process.

It's best to think of the V-Model in terms of the evaluation side first. Evaluation of a particular project moves through different levels of measuring:

- Reaction to the intervention (Level 1)
- Learning; skills and knowledge gained (Level 2)
- Behavior change; application of skills and knowledge use (Level 3)
- Impact measures linked to the intervention (Level 4)
- ROI, a comparison of monetary benefits to the cost of the intervention (Level 5).

From the viewpoint of key stakeholders, such as the clients or sponsors, the higher levels represent increased value, as most clients want to see the business contribution (Level 4) and even sometimes ROI (Level 5). In terms of evaluation of the intervention, it

FIGURE 3-1. Alignment With the V-Model

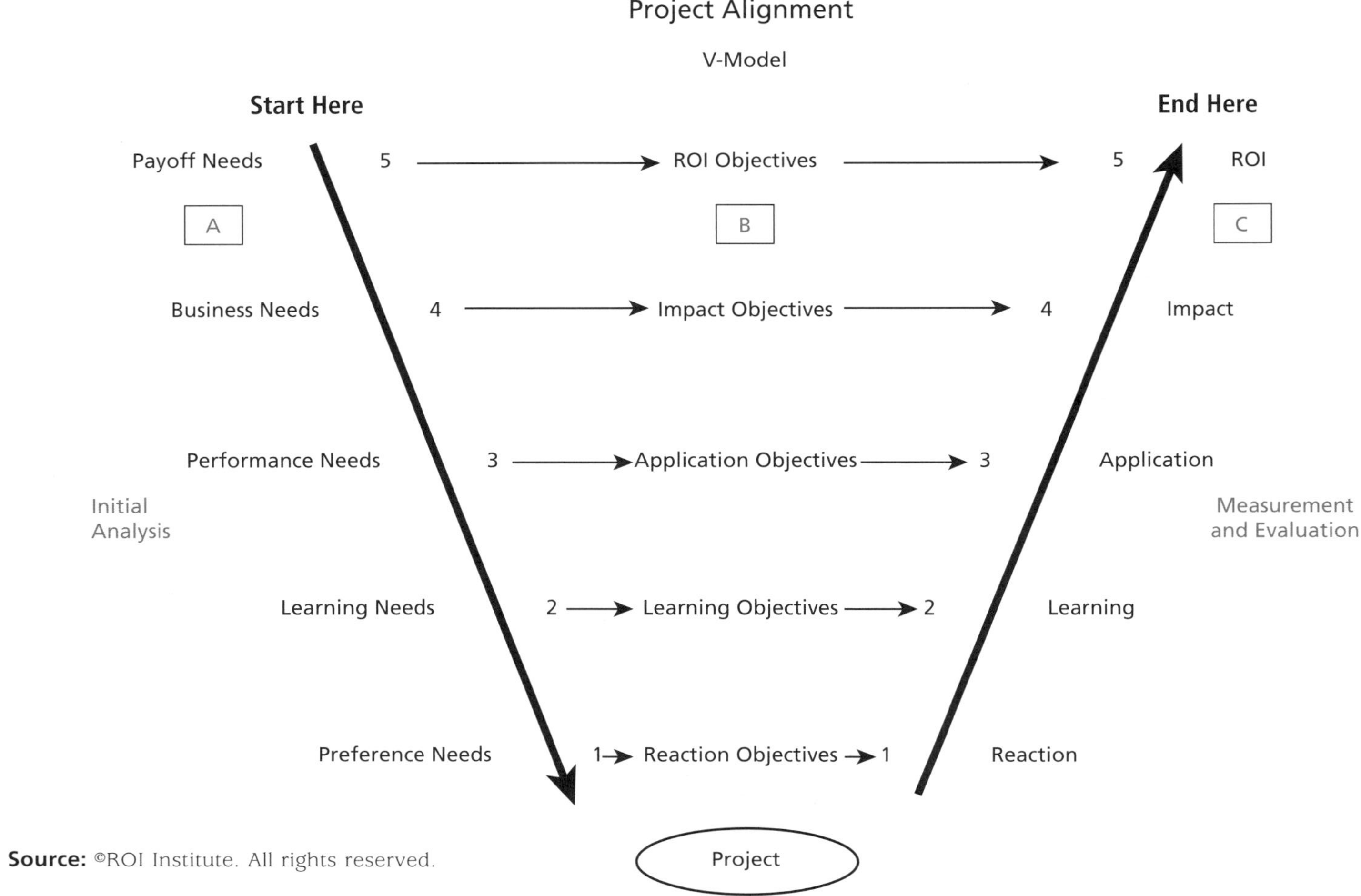

Source: ©ROI Institute. All rights reserved.

is at Level 4 that an isolation technique is applied to specify how much improvement is directly from the intervention. This step ensures that business alignment is confirmed.

The measures that are captured at each level are defined in the objectives. There are five corresponding levels of objectives, as illustrated in Figure 3-1. The objectives increase in value as the levels progress, with Levels 4 and 5 often being the most valuable from a client's perspective. These objectives are developed during the needs assessment. The needs assessment defines particular needs at each level. Here, the highest and most important level is the potential payoff of the intervention, followed by business needs, performance needs, learning needs, and preference needs.

Level 5, Payoff Needs

Needs assessment occurring at Level 5 addresses the potential payoff opportunity for an organization. This step examines the possibility for a return on investment before the intervention is pursued. The first part of the process is to determine if the problem is worth solving or if the opportunity warrants serious consideration. In some cases, this is obvious when there are serious problems that are affecting the organization's operations and strategy. For example, at a hospital, an annual turnover rate of critical talent at 32 percent is an obvious payoff opportunity. Another example is an organization where new account growth is flat and customer loyalty is low, based on industry standards. These types of payoff opportunities make it clear that there is a problem that needs to be solved or an opportunity that should be pursued with a clearly identified business need.

Some requests represent not-so-obvious payoff opportunities, such as a request to implement a succession management process. When this is the case, the business measures of importance become more evident during analysis at Level 4.

During analysis at Level 5, it is important not only to identify the business measures that need to improve, when possible, but also to convert them into monetary values so the anticipated economic benefit of addressing the opportunity is evident. The monetary value of the payoff is useful not only in identifying the scope of the opportunity, but also in forecasting the potential ROI. Once the solution(s) is identified and targets for improvement as a result of the solution are set, it is important to determine an approximate cost for the entire project. With the approximate project cost and the monetary value of the opportunity in hand, you can forecast the ROI in order to indicate the potential payoff for investing in a particular solution. While this practice may not be feasible for some projects, it is often important with very expensive, strategic, or critical projects.

Level 4, Business Needs

At Level 4, business data that indicate movement toward addressing the payoff need are examined to determine which measures are in most need of improvement. This involves a review of HR and organizational databases, examining all types of hard and soft data. It is usually the performance of one of the data items that triggers the consulting project. For example, when market share is not as much as it should be, operating costs are excessive, product quality is deteriorating, or productivity is low, the business measure is easily pinpointed. These are key measures that come directly from the data in the organization and are often found in the operating databases.

Business needs are sometimes arranged in categories of hard data to include output, quality, cost, and time. Examples are sales, production, errors, waste, accidental costs, downtime, project time, and compliance fines. These measures exist in any type of organization, even in the public sector and among nonprofits and nongovernment organizations (NGOs). These measures often attract the attention of executives and chief administrators, as they represent business impact. An important goal is to connect the project to one or more of these measures.

Sometimes, impact measures are subjective, such as customer service, image, work climate, customer satisfaction, job satisfaction, engagement, reputation, and teamwork. Typical HR measures, as shown in Figure 3-2, are examples of soft measures that may be relevant for an OD intervention. Although these measures are not as objectively based as measures of output, quality, cost, and time, they are still important, and in many cases are the primary measures of interest for an OD project. Soft data are sometimes reported as intangible benefits of a project or intervention because they cannot always be converted to money credibly or with a minimum amount of resources. But, they can nonetheless be important business measures that, if improved, can help an organization take advantage of a payoff opportunity.

Level 3, Performance Needs

The Level 3 analysis involves determining performance needs or gaps that if addressed will contribute to improvement in the business measures. The task is to determine what is causing the problem (or creating the opportunity) identified at Level 4 (for example, what is causing the business to be below the desired level?). What should the organization be doing more or less of? Is there something the organization should be doing differently? Performance tools or systems, inadequate technology, and broken or ineffective processes are all examples of performance needs.

The desired state and the current state should reveal performance needs. The reason for the inadequate performance is the basis for the solution or the project. For example, if customer complaints have increased, and it is discovered that the technology used by customer service is outdated and slow, then the technology that supports customer service representatives is the cause of the problem and needs to be resolved.

FIGURE 3-2. Linking OD to HR Measures

Classic HR measures are relevant for OD effectiveness and for a variety of OD projects. Typically, these are:

- talent retention, turnover, and turnover costs
- employee engagement
- job satisfaction
- employee complaints
- absenteeism
- recruitment and onboarding costs
- internal fill rate and time to fill
- utilization rate.

Performance needs can be uncovered using a variety of problem-solving or analysis techniques. This may involve the use of data collection techniques discussed in this book, such as surveys, questionnaires, focus groups, or interviews. Regardless of the technique, the key is to determine all of the causes of the problem so that solutions can be developed. Sometimes one solution can address the performance need; other times there are multiple solutions and then a decision must be made as to which one to pursue if pursuing all is not an option. ROI forecasting is one way to help make the decision.

Level 2, Learning Needs

During the Level 2 learning needs assessment, the specific information, knowledge, or skills that are required to address the performance needs are identified. Analysis may reveal learning deficiencies, in terms of knowledge and skills that can contribute to the problem. In other situations, the solution will need a learning component as employees learn how to implement a new process, procedure, or technology. The learning typically involves acquisition of knowledge or the development of skills necessary to improve performance. In some cases, perceptions or attitudes may need to be altered to make the change management intervention successful. The extent of learning required will determine whether formalized training is needed or if more informal, on-the-job methods can be utilized to build the necessary skills and knowledge.

Level 1, Preference Needs

Finally, Level 1 preference needs assessment describes the preferences for the intervention. This involves determining the preferred way in which those involved in the process will need or want it to be implemented. Typical questions that surface are: "Is this important?" "Is this necessary?" and "Is it relevant to me?" Preference needs may involve aspects of implementation, including decisions such as when learning is expected and in what amounts, how it is presented, and the overall time frame. Implementation involves timing, support, expectations, and other key factors.

An example will help illustrate this linkage. Using the V-Model, Figure 3-3 shows an example of linking needs assessment with the evaluation of a project involving a team-based process for developing new products. The target audience is comprised of team members and team leaders. As the figure shows, the first step is to see if the problem is worth pursuing.

These five levels of needs analysis develop a comprehensive profile for determining how best to address an opportunity or problem worth solving. They also serve as the basis for the intervention objectives.

Objectives

Objectives further align an OD initiative with the business by positioning that initiative with end-outcome in mind at every level. The levels of objectives are as follows.

- **Level 0 Input** objectives are those indicators generally tracked in projects, such as number of programs, people affected, hours, and so on. They are categorized as Level 0 because they do not express whether the intervention was effective or not.
- **Level 1 Reaction**, satisfaction, and planned action objectives describe expected immediate satisfaction with the OD intervention. They describe aspects that are important to the success of the intervention, including the relevance of the change and importance of the information or content shared through the process.
- **Level 2 Learning** objectives describe the expected immediate outcomes in terms of knowledge acquisition, skill attainment, awareness, and insights gained through the intervention. These objectives set the stage for transitioning to performance and behavior change.
- **Level 3 Application** objectives describe the expected intermediate outcomes in terms of what behavior change is expected as a result of the intervention. Objectives may target specific steps to be taken or specific behaviors that need to change.
- **Level 4 Impact** objectives define the specific business measures that should improve as a result of the changed behavior. Improvement in these intermediate (and sometimes, long-term) outcomes represent changes in output, quality, cost, and time measures as well as customer satisfaction and employee satisfaction

FIGURE 3-3. Team-Based Process for Developing Products Example With the V-Model

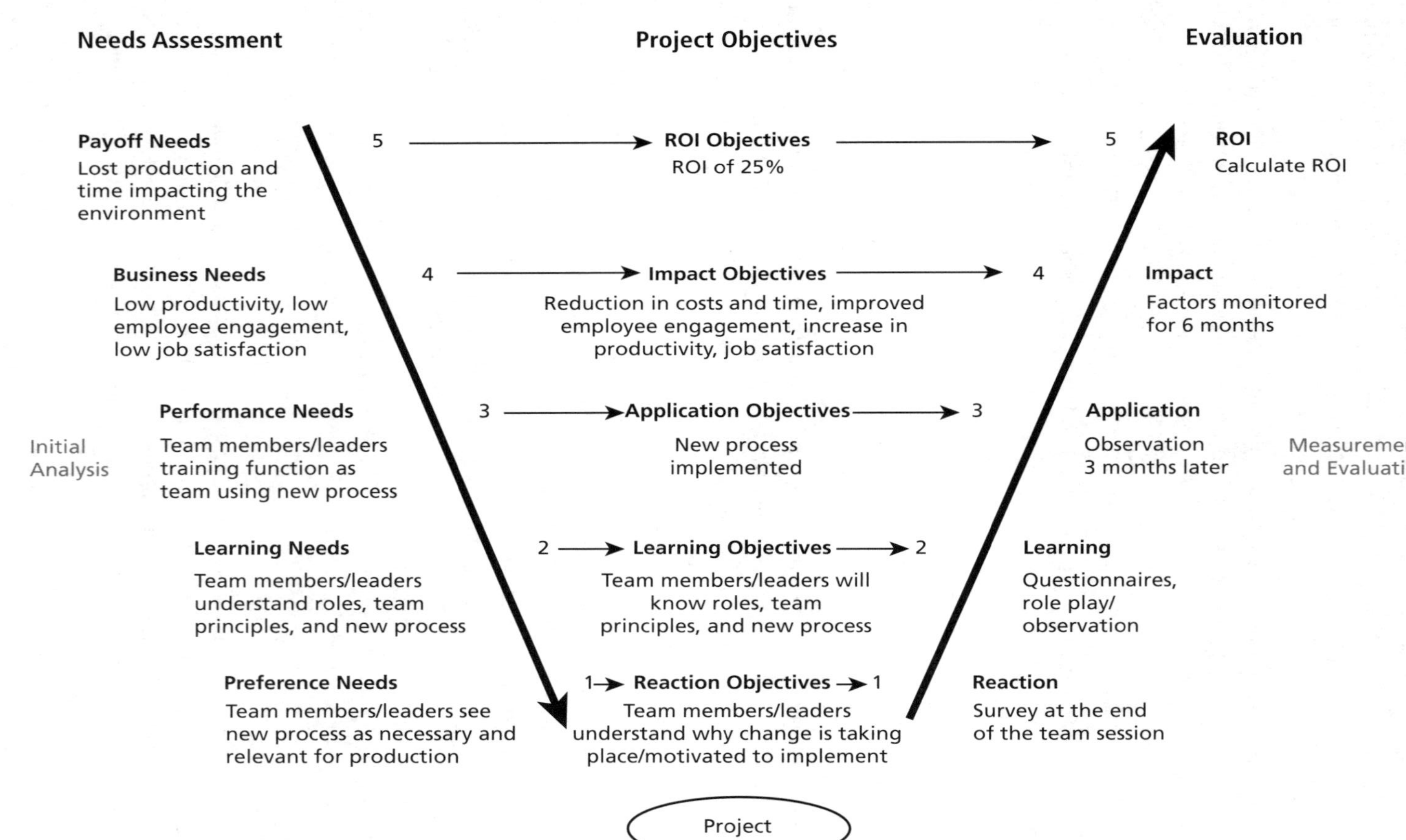

Case in Point

In this example, the payoff need is based on the problem of lost production time and damage caused to the work environment. To understand the impact (Level 4), the problem unfolds with more detail, and it becomes obvious that the problem is worth solving. The average production time has been at an all-time high. Productivity needs to improve; it has not increased in the last 18 months. The pressure of not meeting departmental and organization goals has put stress on employees and has affected job satisfaction and employee engagement. When all these measures are considered, there is clearly a business problem—and to a certain extent, a great opportunity for improvement.

With the confirmation at Level 4 that there are business needs, a potential payoff can be projected. This involves estimating the cost of lost productivity and time. Next, the reduction that can come from the project is determined, using standard values for production and time. This develops a profile of potential payoff and further demonstrates that the problem is worth solving.

At Level 3, the causes of the problem are explored using a variety of techniques. Each measure needs to be analyzed to see what factors are causing its current status (for example, why is productivity not improving, or what is the cause of the job dissatisfaction?). For this project, the analysts conducted interviews and focus groups to understand why business measures were at their current level.

The key principle, as in any diagnostics, is to identify the potential solution to the problem. The new product development process was a viable option for organizing the work in teams. The potential impact was to dramatically reduce the time it took to produce new products. Of course, the intervention also needed to include the soft side as the employee base was not accustomed to working in teams. This meant that the team leaders and team members needed to learn new behaviors that were associated with team performance.

At Level 2, learning is explored. Do team leaders and members understand the new process? Are they clear about their new roles? The new process and team roles are at the heart of the learning needs.

At Level 1, the desired reaction needs to be considered. First, a realistic picture of the change involved must be shared so that teams understand the relevance of this approach. Adapting to change, motivation to implement, and importance of the new process are factors that are critical to the success of launching this approach.

measures. Objectives at this level answer the question, "So what?" as it relates to the intervention. They describe to stakeholders the importance of the intervention.

- **Level 5 ROI** objectives define for stakeholders the intended financial outcome. This single indicator sets the expectation for how the benefits of the OD project will relate to its cost. Before an evaluation is conducted, these objectives must be identified and developed. Ideally, these are developed early in the process when the intervention is designed.

Each level of objective is a category of measures that describe how much progress is being made with addressing the various levels of need. Specific measurable objectives serve as the blueprint for building the OD initiative. By aligning initiatives with the business through a thorough needs assessment and the development of measurable objectives, the implementation and evaluation of an OD initiative become more systematic and reliable. Identifying stakeholder needs and developing relevant objectives are the first two phases of business alignment and set the stage for planning the third phase, evaluation.

EVALUATION PLANNING

Evaluation must be planned—overall and individually—for each initiative. When evaluation is conducted only at reaction levels, not much planning is involved, but as evaluation moves up the value chain, increased attention and efforts need to be placed on planning. During the typical planning cycle, the purpose of evaluation must be reviewed for specific solutions and to determine where the evaluation will stop on the value chain. The feasibility of evaluating at different levels is explored, and two planning documents are developed when the evaluation migrates to application, impact, and ROI: the data collection plan and the data analysis plan. These documents are sometimes used in combination, but are often developed separately.

Planning for Return on Investment Projects

Organization development professionals realize the importance of planning for almost any type of undertaking. Most agree that thorough planning can lead to more effective implementation. The same holds true for ROI analysis. Careful planning for ROI analysis not only saves time and effort, but can also make a difference in the success or failure of the entire project. Planning involves the development of three documents:

1. Data Collection Plan
2. ROI Analysis Plan
3. Communication and Project Plan

These documents are described in detail in the following section. An actual case study is presented here to show how the Data Collection Plan and ROI Analysis Plan are used.

CASE STUDY

A U.S.-based company operates in 12 countries with 21,000 employees. Revenues have increased over the past three years; however, profit margins showed that given the expenses incurred, they were barely breaking even. The company had a solid, loyal customer base and worked hard on gearing their business with what clients needed. What was concerning the executive team was the high turnover rates and low employee satisfaction.

Diagnostics

Recent diagnostics for the main aspects of the business conducted by the OD team determined several key outcomes: 1) employees needed to have a clearer understanding of career paths; 2) to grow the business, more leaders were needed to take positions higher up in the company; 3) the internal fill rate for leadership was 10 percent, and it would be beneficial to the company to groom more internal talent for higher positions. The cost for recruiting from the outside was high and not always effective, particularly in understanding the complexities of the business. Competencies had already been identified for leadership, including communication skills, business acumen, and the ability to align actions to customers' needs.

The OD team linked the competencies to business needs including talent retention, employee satisfaction, internal fill rate, and cost reduction. In the meantime, managers throughout the company were asked to identify high-potential leaders, who based on their performance, would be suitable for leadership. The OD team worked with the executive team and agreed on implementing a 360-degree feedback process, based on the leadership competencies, with the identified high-potential leader group. Due to budgetary constraints, only half of the identified high-potential leader group could go through the 360-degree feedback process in the first year, while the remaining candidates were slated to participate the following year. Based on this fact, the OD team decided to set up this evaluation study as a control group, to isolate the effects of the 360-degree feedback process.

The 360-degree feedback involved several key steps. Before participating, the high- potential leaders participated in a one-hour online session to be familiarized with the process. The 360-degree feedback itself, administered online, collected input from the high-potential leaders themselves, their immediate supervisors, their peers, their direct reports, and in some cases, from customers. This was followed with an OD team member, trained in the assessment, conducting a feedback session along with a comprehensive report for each high-potential leader. An expected outcome was an action plan generated by the high-potential leader and his immediate supervisor.

Objectives

The OD team developed the following multilevel objectives for the intervention:

- Participants will rate the intervention as relevant to their jobs.
- Participants will rate the intervention as important to their career path.
- Participants must demonstrate acceptable performance on each major competency.
- Participants will utilize the competencies with team members on a routine basis.
- Participants will affect cost reduction, increase employee satisfaction, reduce turnover, and increase number of promotions.

Data Collection Plan

Table 3-1 shows the completed data collection plan for a 360-degree feedback assessment intervention. Defining the objectives and measures at each level, including return on investment, is vital. Sometimes, measures can be looked at in different ways, so defining them up front eliminates confusion.

The data collection methods are detailed here to correspond to the different levels of objectives using a range of options described in the next chapter. Next, the data sources are identified. In many cases, data are collected from existing organizational databases. In other cases, data are collected by those participating in the intervention. In some case—as in the case of the 360-degree feedback assessment intervention—high-potential leaders, their immediate supervisors, their peers, their direct reports, and customers provide data.

Timing is important to determine specifically when data are collected from the different sources for each level. During implementation, data often come directly from those involved in the project. In other situations, the follow-up can be determined based on when the intervention is operational and successful.

Finally, the responsibilities are detailed, outlining specifically who will be involved in the data collection process.

ROI Analysis Plan

Table 3-2 shows the completed ROI analysis plan for the same intervention described in Table 3-1. This plan is connected to the previous plan through business impact data. The first column on this plan is the detailed definition of each impact data measure.

The second column defines the method for isolating the effects of the intervention on each data item, using one or more of the specific techniques available. The method of converting data to monetary values is listed in the third column, using one or more available techniques.

The next column defines the cost categories for the specific intervention or solution. Using a fully loaded cost profile, all the categories are detailed here. Completing this action during planning is helpful in determining if specific cost categories need to be monitored during the intervention implementation. The next column defines the intangible benefits that may be derived from this intervention. When listed here, the intangible benefits are only anticipated; they must be measured in some way to determine if they have been influenced by the intervention. Finally, the other influences that may affect implementation are specified along with any additional comments.

Communication and Implementation Plan

The communication and implementation plan details how the results will be communicated to various groups. It also details the specific schedule of events and activities connected to the other planning documents. The targets for communication identify the specific groups that will receive the information. The plan should also include the method of communicating, the content of the communication, and the timing for the communication.

This plan defines the rationale for communicating with the group and for anticipated payoffs, along with the individual responsibility for monitoring actions from the evaluation. It clearly delivers the information to the right groups to ensure that action occurs; in almost every impact study, there are significant actions that can be taken.

FINAL THOUGHTS

This chapter explored alignment of OD projects and evaluation planning. It described in detail when and how ROI analysis should be considered as a process improvement tool. Using the V-Model, a step-by-step explanation was provided to properly align OD projects with business needs. Special attention was paid to integrating OD diagnostics with the ROI Methodology, ensuring the OD practitioner has adequate tools and understanding to conduct needs assessment and plan for the evaluation. Finally, the role of planning for an ROI project was presented, detailing the key steps in the process with the use of an actual case study, illustrating how planning documents are used.

TABLE 3-1. Data Collection Plan

Intervention: 360° Feedback for High-Potential Leaders Responsibility: ____________ Date: ____________

Level	Objective(s)	Measures/Data	Data Collection Method	Data Sources	Timing	Responsibilities
1	**SATISFACTION/PLANNED ACTION** • Relevance to job • Importance to career path and promotion • Action items as a result of 360°	• Average of 4 on 5-point scale	• Questionnaire	• High-potential leaders	• Immediately following receiving 360° feedback	• OD team
2	**LEARNING** • Uncovering strengths/weaknesses • Gaining business acumen • Communicating effectively • Enhancing leadership skills • Improving marketing skills	• Average of 4 on 5-point scale	• Questionnaire	• High-potential leaders	• Immediately following receiving 360° Feedback	• Facilitator
3	**BEHAVIOR CHANGE** • Demonstrate competencies • Utilize the competencies with team members routinely as evidenced by scores on second administration of the 360° feedback	• Checklist for action plan • 4 out of 5 on a 5-point scale	• Action plan • 360° feedback	• High-potential leaders • Supervisors, direct reports, peers	• Six months after 360° feedback, it is administered a second time	• Facilitator • Store Training Coordinator

4	**BUSINESS IMPACT** • Talent retention • Employee satisfaction • Promotion • Cost reduction	• Reduce costs • Decrease in voluntary turnover • Increase in promotion • Increase employee satisfaction	• HR database • Operational database	• High-potential leaders	• Six months after 360° feedback	• Store Training Coordinator
5	**ROI** • 25%	Comments: Action plans are provided and explained during the 360° feedback process. High-potential leaders commit to filling out action plans and sharing copy with OD team.				

TABLE 3-2. ROI Analysis Plan for 360° Feedback Process

Program: 360° Feedback for High-Potential Leaders Responsibility:________________ Date:________________

Data Items (Usually Level 4)	Methods for Isolating the Effects of the Intervention	Methods of Converting Data to Monetary Values	Cost Categories	Intangible Benefits	Communication Targets for Final Report	Other Influences/ Issues During Application	Comments
Cost reduction	Control group	Standard value	• Diagnostics • 360° feedback fees • Time of those involved in process • Administrative overhead • Communication expenses • Facilities • Evaluation	• Increased job satisfaction • Increase in promotion	• Executives • Sponsors • OD team • Prospective participants for 360° feedback	• An initiative that may influence the impact measures is the leadership development programs	

4

Data Collection

Collecting data is like collecting garbage. You've got to know what you're going to do with the stuff before you collect it.

—Mark Twain

For many OD practitioners with psychometrics and industrial psychology in their backgrounds, data collection is based on behavioral science methods. Data collection has relevance throughout the consulting cycle, beginning with diagnostics and ending with post-intervention. The primary objectives of data collection are to systematically gather information at three significant times: 1) before, to understand organization problems and record hypotheses; 2) during, to collect reaction and learning data; and 3) after, to confirm effectiveness of the intervention through collecting application and impact data. Data collection methods, principles, and timing are explored in this chapter. Particular attention is given to collecting data for ROI analysis, and introducing questions to gather estimates for ROI calculation.

QUANTITATIVE AND QUALITATIVE INQUIRY

Advantages to Quantitative Data

There are advantages and disadvantages to both quantitative and qualitative methods of research. Quantitative results have the advantage of being able to provide numerical value for large amounts of data as well as permitting the use of more powerful methods of mathematical and statistical analysis. Some people argue that the only data are quantitative data. They posit that everything is either a 0 or 1. Quantitative data can help form conclusions by assigning value from attributes to numerical scales and defined categories, and it is more easily analyzed with the use of software systems such as Excel or SPSS.

Advantages to Qualitative Data

Qualitative data also has advantages, such as by allowing clients to use their own words to describe organization factors and problems. This method is helpful in situations where the practitioner has a general sense of what to look for, but does not know details or specifics about an organization. That is why OD practitioners find qualitative interviews and focus groups particularly helpful in the beginning of a project. Qualitative data provide richness, depth, and complexity that may be unique to the organization culture. It is important to consider culture and its implication for data collection.

Organization Culture Implications

Organization culture may have implications for data collection methods. For some organizations, surveys are considered impersonal and bothersome. Some organizations are notorious for constantly surveying employees with no clear thought around the timing and methods for collecting data. Other organizations may be feedback deprived. This observation alone may be worth exploring, as there may be underlying assumptions about means of communication within the organization.

Another consideration that relates to organization culture is providing confidential or anonymous surveys. Online surveys allow for anonymity in providing input. Anonymity could be a critical point to consider in the context of organization culture. Some groups have found that by offering anonymous questionnaires, it not only helps to improve response rates, but provides richer and more comprehensive data.

Mixing It Up

Mixed methodology allows for a combined qualitative/quantitative approach. This tactic is used often in creating a questionnaire. In this case, the qualitative method precedes the quantitative, by gathering important details that will help form the questions and response options for the questionnaire. For example, an OD practitioner working for a European cellular company conducted customer interviews to collect customer-specific perceptions and feedback. Once the interview data were organized and analyzed, the OD practitioner created a questionnaire based on the interview findings. In this way, the hypotheses could be confirmed and helped to target the questionnaire to gather generalizable findings.

Resource Implications

Many companies today rely on quantitative methods, as data collection and analysis processes are automated with the use of online-hosted survey systems. This implies more up-front work to create meaningful questions, but in the cases with simple analysis and reporting, automating this process can drastically reduce the effort. Questionnaires also allow the practitioner to collect sample data that are representative of the populations, and with proper analytical tools, infer generalizations about the larger population or organization as a whole.

DATA COLLECTION METHODS

Questionnaires and Surveys

The most common method of data collection is the questionnaire. Ranging from short reaction forms to detailed follow-up tools, questionnaires are used to obtain subjective information about the organization or group involved, as well as objective data to measure business results for ROI analysis. With its versatility and popularity, the questionnaire is an optimal method for capturing the first four levels of data (reaction, learning, application, and business impact). Surveys represent a specific type of questionnaire to capture attitudes, beliefs, and opinions. The principles of survey construction and design are similar to questionnaire design. A questionnaire may include any of the following types of items:

- An *open-ended question* has an unlimited answer. The question is followed by ample blank space for the response.
- A *checklist* provides a list of items where respondents are asked to check those that apply in the situation.
- A *two-way question* has alternate responses (yes/no) or other possibilities.
- A *multiple-choice question* asks the respondent to select the one most applicable response.
- A *ranking scale* requires the respondent to rank a list of items.

Questionnaire design is a straightforward, logical process. Table 4-1 shows the steps that help develop a valid, reliable, and effective instrument.

Questionnaire Content for Different Levels

The areas of feedback used on reaction questionnaires depend on the purpose of the evaluation. Some forms are simple, while others are detailed and require considerable time to complete. When a comprehensive evaluation is planned, and impact and ROI are being measured, the reaction questionnaire can be simple, asking only questions that provide pertinent information about an individual's perception of the intervention. However, when a reaction questionnaire is the only means of collecting evaluation data, then a more comprehensive list of questions is necessary. This feedback can be useful in making adjustments to an organization and assisting in predicting performance after the intervention, or both.

In most medium to large organizations with significant OD interventions, reaction instruments are automated for analysis and reporting. Some organizations use direct input into a website to develop detailed reports as well as databases, which allows feedback data to be compared to other interventions.

TABLE 4-1. Questionnaire Design Steps

1. Determine the specific information needed for each domain or level.
2. Secure input from subject matter experts.
3. Involve management in the process, when appropriate and feasible.
4. Decide on the method for returning the questionnaire.
5. Select the type(s) of questions. Keep in mind the time needed for analysis.
6. Choose the first question carefully.
7. Group related questions.
8. Begin with easy questions and build to the more complex.
9. Present the questions in the order of the results chain of impact.
10. Place sensitive questions at the end of the questionnaire.
11. Develop the questions with clarity and simplicity in mind.
12. Draft the questionnaire, checking the flow and total length.
13. Check the reading level and match it to the audience.
14. Design for ease of tabulation and analysis.
15. Be consistent in the visual presentation of the questions.
16. Use color and contrast to help respondents recognize the components of the questionnaire without distracting from the items themselves.
17. Avoid clutter and complexity in the question.
18. Develop the revised questionnaire.
19. Test the questions with a small group of individuals who are knowledgeable about the target audience.
20. Keep responses anonymous or confidential.
21. Finalize the completed questionnaire and prepare a data summary.
22. Use an existing user-friendly software tool, if feasible.

Collecting learning data with a questionnaire is also common. Simple questions to measure learning can be developed to include in the reaction questionnaire or in the form of a test.

Possible areas to explore on a questionnaire aimed at measuring learning are:

- change in perception or attitude
- knowledge gain
- skill enhancement
- ability
- capability
- awareness.

Questions to gauge learning are developed using a format similar to the reaction part of the questionnaire. They measure the extent to which learning has taken place.

Questionnaires are also commonly used to collect post-intervention application and impact data. Table 4-2 presents a list of questionnaire content possibilities for capturing these follow-up data. Reaction and learning data may also be captured in a follow-up questionnaire to compare to similar data gathered immediately following the intervention. Most follow-up issues, however, involve application and implementation (Level 3) and business impact (Level 4).

TABLE 4-2. Typical Content Areas for Post-Intervention Questionnaires

• Use of materials, guides, and technology
• Application of knowledge/skills
• Frequency of use of knowledge/skills
• Success with use of knowledge/skills
• Change in work or work behavior
• Improvements/accomplishments
• Monetary impact of improvements
• Improvements linked to the intervention
• Confidence level of data supplied
• Perceived value of the investment
• Linkage with output measures
• Barriers to implementation
• Enablers to implementation
• Management support for implementation
• Other benefits
• Other possible solutions
• Target audience recommendations

Testing

Testing can be important for measuring learning in OD intervention evaluations. Pre- and post-intervention tests are an effective way to measure the change in learning. An improvement in test scores shows the change in skill, knowledge, or attitude attributed to the intervention. Performance testing, simulations, role-plays, and business games are used to measure the extent of skill gained related to an intervention.

Interviews

Another helpful data collection method is the interview. The OD team or a third party usually conducts the interviews. Interviews can secure data not available in business or organization databases or data that may be difficult to obtain through written responses or observations. Also, interviews can uncover success stories that can be useful in communicating evaluation results. Organization members may be reluctant to describe their results in a questionnaire, but they may be willing to volunteer the information to a skillful interviewer who uses probing techniques. The interview process can uncover reaction, learning, and impact data, but it is primarily used during diagnostics and post-intervention phases. It is particularly useful with gathering application or performance data. A major disadvantage of the interview is that it is time-consuming, since it requires interviewer preparation to ensure the process is consistent, as well as the interviewer conducting thematic analysis afterwards.

Interviews are categorized into two basic types: structured and unstructured. A structured interview is much like a questionnaire. The interviewer asks specific questions that allow the interviewee little room to deviate from the menu of expected responses. The structured interview offers several advantages over the questionnaire. For example, an interview can ensure that the questions are answered and that the interviewer understands the responses supplied by the interviewee. The unstructured interview has built-in flexibility to allow the interviewer to probe for additional information. This type of interview uses a handful of core questions, which can lead to more detailed information as important data are uncovered. The interviewer must be skilled in interviewing a variety of individuals and using the probing process. Interview design and steps for interviews are similar to those of the questionnaire. Preparing the interviewer, piloting the interview, providing clear instruction to the interviewee, and asking a set of core questions are critical steps in gathering useful data.

Focus Groups

Similar to interviews, focus groups are helpful when in-depth feedback is needed. The focus group involves a small group discussion conducted by an experienced facilitator. It solicits qualitative feedback on a planned topic. Group members are all invited to provide their thoughts, as individual input builds on group input.

Focus groups have several advantages over questionnaires, surveys, tests, or interviews. The basic premise of using focus groups is that when quality perspectives are subjective, several individual perspectives are better than one. The group process, whereby group members stimulate ideas in others, is an effective method for generating qualitative data. Focus groups are less expensive than individual interviews and can be quickly planned and conducted. They should be small (eight to 12 individuals) and should consist of a representative sample of the target population. Group facilitators should have expertise in conducting focus groups with a wide range of individuals. The flexibility of this data collection method makes it possible to explore organizational matters before the intervention as well as to collect post-intervention's unexpected outcomes or application. Barriers to implementation can also be explored through focus groups, while collecting examples and real concerns from those involved in the intervention.

Focus groups are particularly helpful when qualitative information is needed about the success of an intervention. For example, focus groups can be used in the following ways:

- to collect information contributing to diagnosis and proposed solution
- to gauge the overall effectiveness of intervention application
- to identify the barriers and enablers to a successful implementation
- to isolate the impact of an organization from other influences.

Essentially, focus groups are helpful when evaluation information is needed but cannot be collected adequately with questionnaires, interviews, or quantitative methods. The focus group is an inexpensive and quick way to determine the strengths and weaknesses of HR interventions. For a complete evaluation, focus group information should be combined with data from other instruments.

Observations

Another potentially useful data collection method is observation. The observer may be a member of the OD team, an immediate manager, a member of a peer group, or an external party. The most common observer, and probably the most practical, is a member of the OD team.

To be effective, observations need to be systematic and well developed, minimizing the observer's influence and subjectivity. Observers should be carefully selected, fully prepared, and knowledgeable about how to interpret, score (if relevant), and report what they see.

This method is useful for collecting data on leadership development, employee training, coaching, and performance evaluation. For example, observation is used to provide 360-degree feedback as behavior changes are solicited from the direct reports, colleagues, internal customers, immediate managers, and self-input. This is considered a delayed report method of observation. This feedback process can be the actual intervention, or could be used before participating in another development initiative.

There are cases when observation is either invisible or unnoticeable. *Invisible* means that the person under observation is not aware that the observation is taking place, as in the case of a secret shopper. For example, Starbucks uses secret shoppers to observe their employees. A secret shopper goes to one of the stores, takes note of how long orders take to process, the demeanor of the server, whether the store and bathrooms are clean, and whether the server is familiar with new drink offerings. But the observation continues immediately following the visit when the secret shopper goes and takes temperature checks of his drink order. All of this observation activity is supposed to be done in a way unbeknownst to the server. Another type of observation is *unnoticeable*, which means that although the person under observation may know that the observation is taking place, he does not notice it because it occurs over a longer period of time or at random times, as in listening in on customer service calls (*this call may be monitored for quality assurance purposes*), or in the case of a 360-degree feedback process.

Action Plans and Performance Agreements

For many OD interventions, business data are readily available to the OD team. However, at times data won't be easily accessible to the intervention evaluator. Sometimes, data are maintained at the individual, work unit, or department level and may not be known to anyone outside that area. Tracking down those data sets may be too expensive and time-consuming. In these cases, the use of action plans and performance agreements may be helpful in capturing data sets.

Action plans capture application and implementation data; however, this method can also be a useful way to collect business impact data. For business impact data, the action plan is more focused and often deemed more credible than a questionnaire. We define the performance agreement as essentially an action plan with a pre-intervention commitment. An action plan can easily be converted to a performance agreement with minor adjustments. The main difference between an action plan and a performance agreement is that performance agreements put the dialogue and agreement between a group member and his immediate manager. This can be a powerful process that can drive tremendous results, and is appropriate for OD interventions where there is a need to achieve improvement. Not only do group members have the content to drive improvement but they also will have the support of their immediate managers and the extra efforts and attention of the facilitator to meet the performance target.

The basic design principles involved in developing and administering action plans are the same for collecting both application and business impact data. The following steps are recommended when an action plan is developed and implemented to capture business impact data and to convert the data to monetary values. The adjustments needed to convert action plans to performance agreements are described at the end of the section.

Set Goals and Targets

As shown in Figure 4-1, an action plan can be developed with a direct focus on business impact data. The plan presented in this figure requires an overall objective for the plan to be developed, which is usually the primary objective of the intervention. In some cases, an organization may have more than one objective, which requires additional action plans. In addition to the objective, the improvement measure is defined, along with the current and target levels of performance. This information requires that the individual anticipates the application of skills and sets goals for specific performances that can be realized.

The action plan is completed during the intervention, often with input and assistance from an OD practitioner. The practitioner actually approves the plan, indicating that the action steps meet the requirements of being SMART: **s**pecific, **m**otivating, **a**chievable, **r**ealistic, and **t**ime-based. Each plan can be developed in a 30-minute time frame and often begins with action steps related to the intervention. These action steps are Level 3 activities that detail application and implementation of intervention content. All these steps build support for and are linked to business impact measures.

Simplicity Rules the Day! Defining the Unit of Measure

The next step is to define the actual unit of measure. In some cases, more than one measure may be used and will subsequently be contained in additional action plans. The unit of measure is necessary to break the process into the simplest steps so that its ultimate value can be determined. The unit may be output data, such as one unit produced or one closed sale. In terms of quality, the unit can be one reject, one error, or one re-work. Time-based units are usually measured in minutes, hours, days, or weeks, such as one hour of process time. Other units are specific to their particular type of data, such as one grievance, one complaint, one absence, or one turnover. Here, simplicity rules the day by breaking down impact data into the simplest terms possible.

Place a Monetary Value on Each Improvement

During the intervention, those involved are asked to locate, calculate, or estimate the monetary value for each improvement outlined in their plans. The unit value is determined using a variety of methods such as standard values, expert input, external databases, or estimates.

The process used in arriving at the value is described in the instructions for the action plan. When the actual improvement occurs, these values will be used to capture the annual monetary benefits of the plan. In the worst-case scenario, those participating in the OD intervention are asked to estimate the value. When estimates are necessary, it is important to collect the basis of their calculations. Space for this

FIGURE 4-1. Sample Intervention Action Plan

Name:__________ Facilitator Signature__________ Follow-Up Date__________ Objective: __________

Evaluation Period __________ to__________ Improvement Measure: __________

Current Performance __________ Target Performance__________

Action Steps	Analysis
1. __________	A. What is the unit of measure? __________
2. __________	B. What is the value (cost) of one unit? $__________
3. __________	C. How did you arrive at this value? __________
4. __________	D. How much did the measure change during the evaluation period? (monthly value) __________
5. __________	E. List the other factors that have influenced this change. __________
6. __________	
7. __________	
Intangible Benefits:	F. What percent of this change was actually caused by this program? __________%
	G. What level of confidence do you place on the above information? (100%=Certainty and 0%=No Confidence) __________%

Comments: __________

information should be provided. The preferred actions are using standard values or an expert. Also, the OD practitioner must be prepared to discuss values and reasonable methods in the session.

Implement the Action Plan

Ideally, the action plan is implemented post-intervention. Action plan steps are followed (Level 3), and subsequent business impact improvements are ensured (Level 4). The results are forwarded to the OD team.

Provide Specific Improvements

At the end of the specified follow-up period—usually three months, six months, nine months, or one year—group members indicate the specific improvements made, usually expressed as a daily, weekly, or monthly amount. This determines the actual amount of change that has been observed, measured, and recorded. Group members must understand the need for accuracy as data are recorded. In most cases, only the changes are recorded, as those amounts are needed to calculate the monetary values linked to the intervention. In other cases, before and after data may be recorded, which allows the evaluator to calculate the differences.

Isolate the Effects of the Intervention

Although the action plan is initiated because of the intervention, the actual improvements reported on the action plan may be influenced by other factors. The intervention usually shares the credit for the improvement gained. For example, an action plan to implement leadership skills for department managers could only be given partial credit for a business improvement because other variables in the work unit might have influenced the impact measures. While several ways are available to isolate the effects of an intervention, group member estimation is often used in the action planning process. Group members are asked to estimate the percentage of the improvement directly related to the intervention. This question can be asked on the action plan form or in a follow-up questionnaire, as sometimes it's beneficial to precede this question with a request to identify all the other factors that might have influenced the results. This allows group members to think through the relationships before allocating a portion to this intervention. Additional detail on methods to isolate the effects of interventions is presented in chapter 5.

Provide a Confidence Level for Estimates

Isolating the amount of the improvement directly related to the intervention is not a precise process. Because it is an estimate, an error adjustment is made. Group members are asked to indicate their levels of confidence in their estimates using a scale of 0 to 100 percent—where 0 percent means no confidence and 100 percent means the estimates represent absolute certainty. The confidence estimate serves as an error discount factor.

Collect Action Plans

An excellent response rate is essential, so several steps may be necessary to ensure that the action plans are completed and returned. Usually, group members will see the importance of the process and develop their plans during the intervention. Some organizations use follow-up reminders by mail or email. Others call group members to check progress. Still others offer assistance in developing the final plan. These steps may require additional resources, which need to be weighed against the importance of having more precise data. Specific ways to improve response rates are discussed later in this chapter.

Summarize the Data and Calculate the Return on Investment

If developed properly, each action plan will have annualized monetary values associated with improvements. Also, each individual will indicate the percentage of the improvement directly related to the intervention. Finally, group members will have provided a confidence estimate expressed as a percentage to reflect their uncertainty with the estimates and the subjective nature of some of the data they provided.

Because this process involves estimates, it may not appear to be accurate. Several adjustments during the analysis make the process credible and more accurate. These adjustments reflect the guiding principles of the ROI Methodology, and are outlined as steps 1-6 below.

Step 1: For those group members who do not provide data, the assumption is that they had no improvement to report. This is a very conservative approach.

Step 2: Each value is checked for realism, usability, and feasibility. Extreme values are discarded and omitted from the analysis.

Step 3: Because improvement is annualized, the assumption is that the intervention had no improvement after the first year (for short-term interventions). Some add value in years two and three.

Step 4: The new values are adjusted by the percentage of the improvement related directly to the intervention using multiplication. This isolates the effects of the intervention.

Step 5: The improvement from step 4 is then adjusted using the confidence estimate, multiplying it by the confidence percentage. The confidence estimate is actually an error percentage suggested by the group participants. The confidence estimate is multiplied by the amount of improvement connected to the intervention.

For example:

- A group participant indicates 80 percent confidence reflecting a 20 percent error possibility (100 – 80 = 20).
- In a $10,000 estimate with an 80 percent confidence factor, the group participant suggests that the value can be in the range of $8,000 to $12,000 (20 percent less to 20 percent more).
- To be conservative, the lower number, $8,000, is used.

Step 6: The monetary values determined in the previous five steps are totaled to arrive at the final intervention benefit. Since these values are already annualized, the total of these benefits becomes the annual benefits for the intervention. This value is placed in the numerator of the ROI formula to calculate the return on investment.

Improving the Response Rate for Data Collection

One of the greatest challenges in data collection is achieving an acceptable response rate. Requiring too much information may result in a suboptimal response rate. The challenge, therefore, is to tackle data collection design and administration so as to achieve maximum response rate. This is critical when the primary data collection method hinges on input obtained through questionnaires, surveys, and action plans. Table 4-3 shows 16 ways to boost response rates.

SOURCES OF DATA

An array of possible data sources is available to provide input on the success of an OD intervention. Six general categories are described here.

Business and Operational Databases

Perhaps the most useful and credible data sources for impact and ROI analysis are the databases and reports of the organization. Whether individualized or group-based, these records reflect performance in a work unit, department, division, region, or overall organization. Organization databases include all types of measures and are a preferred way to collect data for impact and ROI evaluation because these data sets usually reflect business impact data and are relatively easy to obtain. However, the old adage, "*garbage in, garbage out*," rings true here. Inconsistent and inaccurate data entry and data processing steps may complicate the task of usefulness.

TABLE 4-3. Ways to Increase Response Rates

• Provide advance communication about the questionnaire.
• Clearly communicate the reason for the questionnaire.
• Indicate who will see the results of the questionnaire.
• Show how the data will be integrated with other data.
• Keep the questionnaire as simple as possible.
• Keep questionnaire responses anonymous—or at least confidential.
• Make it easy to respond with email.
• Use two follow-up reminders.
• Have the introduction letter signed by a top executive.
• Send a summary of results to target audience.
• Have a third party collect and analyze data.
• Communicate the time limit for submitting responses.
• Design questionnaire to attract attention, with a professional format.
• Let group members know what actions will be taken with the data.
• Provide options to respond (e.g. paper-based).
• Frame questions so group members can respond appropriately to relevant questions.

Intervention Group Members

Perhaps the most widely used data source for an ROI analysis is from those participating in the OD intervention. Group members are frequently asked about reaction (Level 1), learning (Level 2), and how skills, knowledge, and procedures have been applied on the job (Level 3). Sometimes they are asked to explain the impact or consequence of those actions. Group members are a rich source of data for evaluation at the first four levels of data.

Group members are credible because they are involved in the intervention and are expected to make it successful. Also, they know the most about other factors that may influence results. The challenge is to find an effective, efficient, and consistent way to capture data from this important source to minimize the time required to provide input.

Group Members' Immediate Managers

Another important data source is the immediate supervisors of the group members. Managers often have a vested interest in the evaluation process because they approve, support, or require the group members to become involved in the intervention in the first place. In many situations, they observe the group members as they attempt to make the intervention successful by applying their new learning.

Because of this, the managers are able to report on the successes linked to the intervention, as well as the difficulties and problems associated with application. Although manager input is usually best for application evaluation (Level 3), it is sometimes helpful for impact (Level 4) evaluation. The challenge is to make data collection convenient, efficient, and not disruptive.

Direct Reports

Because most OD interventions involve supervisors, managers, and executives, their direct reports can be important sources of data. Direct reports can report perceived changes since the intervention was implemented. Input from direct reports is usually appropriate for application (Level 3) data. For example, in a 360-degree feedback intervention, comments from direct reports are perhaps the most credible source of data for changes in leadership behavior.

Team/Peer Group

Individuals who serve as team members or occupy peer-level positions in the organization are a source of data for some interventions. Team/peer group members are usually a source of input for 360-degree feedback. In these situations, peer group members provide input on perceived changes since the intervention has been implemented. This source is appropriate when all team members participate in the intervention and, consequently, when they can report on the collective efforts of the group.

Internal/External Groups

In some situations, internal or external groups such as the OD team, intervention facilitators, coaches, mentors, expert observers, or external consultants may provide input on the success of the individuals when they learn and apply the skills and knowledge covered in the intervention. Sometimes expert observers or assessors may be used to measure learning. This source may be useful for on-the-job application (Level 3).

TIMING FOR DATA COLLECTION

Another important factor is the timing of data collection. In some cases, pre-change measurements are taken to compare with post-change measures, or multiple measures are taken. In other situations, pre-change measures are not available and specific follow-ups are still taken after the program. The important issue is to determine the timing for the follow-up evaluation.

The timing of data collection can vary. When a follow-up evaluation is planned after the intervention, determining the best time for data collection is critical. The challenge is to analyze the nature and scope of the application and implementation and determine the earliest time that a trend or pattern will evolve. This occurs when the application of skills becomes routine and the implementation is progressing properly. Deciding when to collect data often involves knowing the audience and general time it takes to see change. Collecting data as early as possible is important so that potential adjustments can still be made. At the same time, evaluations must allow for behavior changes to occur, so that the application of skills can be observed and measured. Two factors will usually determine the routine use of skills: the complexity of the skill and the opportunity to use the skill. In interventions spanning a considerable length of time for implementation, measures may be taken at three- to six-month intervals. This provides successive input on progress and clearly shows the extent of improvement, using effective measures at well-timed intervals.

The timing for impact data collection is based on the delay between application and consequence (the impact). Subject matter experts familiar with this situation will have to examine the content of the application and implementation and, when considering the context of the work environment, estimate how long it will take for the application to have an impact. In some situations, such as the use of new tools or procedures, the impact may immediately follow the application; in other processes, such as the use of complex leadership skills, the impact may be delayed for some time. For example, managers involved in an OD effort to improve talent retention will have to learn to work more closely with the team, demonstrating increased caring for the group; assisting team members in achieving individual and professional goals; providing challenging assignments; and allowing team members to learn, grow, and develop. A mere change of behavior will not necessarily result in an immediate reduction in turnover of critical talent. There will be some lag between the new behavior and the corresponding increase in retention; however, the impact will usually occur in the time frame of one to six months in most OD interventions. The key is to move as quickly as possible to collect the impact data as soon as it occurs.

Convenience and constraints also influence the timing of data collection. Perhaps the group members are conveniently meeting in a follow-up session or at a special event. These would be excellent opportunities to collect data. Sometimes constraints are placed on data collection. Sponsors or other executives are eager to have the data, to make decisions about the intervention. So they move data collection to an earlier-than-ideal time. If it's too early, another, later data collection will be necessary.

Management's Time for Data Input

The time that a group member's immediate manager must allocate to data collection is another important issue when selecting a data collection method. Always strive to keep the managers' time requirements to a minimum. Some methods, such as focus groups, may require involvement from the manager prior to and after the intervention. Other methods, such as performance monitoring, may not require any manager time.

Disruption of Normal Work Activities

Another important factor in data collection is the amount of disruption created by the method selected. Routine work processes should be disrupted as little as possible. Some data collection techniques, such as business or operational databases, require little time or distraction from normal activities. Questionnaires generally do not disrupt the work environment and can often be completed in only a few minutes or even after normal work hours. Techniques such as focus group and interviews may take more time for those involved.

Accuracy of Method

Accuracy is a factor to weigh when selecting a data collection method. Accuracy refers to the instrument's or the method's ability to correctly capture the data desired, with minimum error. Some data collection methods are more accurate than others. For example, organization databases tend to be more accurate than an interview. If data are needed regarding on-the-job behavior, unobtrusive observation is a powerful option.

FINAL THOUGHTS

This chapter has provided an overview of data collection methods that can be used in ROI analysis. OD practitioners and evaluators have the option to select from a variety of methods according to their resources, culture, and circumstances. Follow-up questionnaires and surveys are commonly used to collect data for application and impact analyses. Questionnaire design and ways to boost response rates were also explored. In the OD field, the use of action plans and performance agreements can be very effective. Next up, data analysis...after the data are collected, what do you do with it?

5

Data Analysis

It is a capital mistake to theorize before one has data.

—Arthur Conan Doyle

Most OD practitioners will agree that data analysis and interpretation is one of the most challenging tasks of measurement and evaluation. A misunderstanding of the techniques as well as a fear of math and statistics confounds this challenge. This chapter describes five key steps in simple terms.

The first part of the chapter addresses isolating the impact of an OD intervention. In almost every situation, other variables will influence the impact of an OD intervention and these factors must be taken into account.

The second part of the chapter discusses converting data to monetary values. It is one thing to collect the data, but it is a different process to assign a monetary value to it.

The third part of the chapter is on the cost of the intervention. Since the ROI formula has two numbers—one is cost and the other is benefit—we will look at the key elements to include when calculating the costs of OD interventions.

The fourth part focuses on calculating the return on investment (ROI), and presents common approaches to calculate values that can be used in comparison with other types of investment.

The final section is on intangibles, the impact measures that are not converted to money. Refer back to Figure 2-2 in chapter 2 for a visual depiction of the steps.

ISOLATING THE EFFECTS

The situation is not uncommon. Some type of improvement is noted after a major OD intervention has been implemented. The two events appear to be related. Somebody asks, "How much of this improvement was due to the OD intervention?" While this question is often asked, it is rarely answered with any degree of certainty. While the change in performance may be related to the intervention, other factors may also have contributed to the improvement. The intervention is only one of many variables that can influence performance. This section explores several techniques that can be used to answer the question, "What impact did the OD intervention have on performance?" with a much greater degree of certainty. Taking the time to carry out this step creates additional credibility for the process by focusing attention on other variables that may have influenced performance. In the following section, we will describe the isolation techniques we have used with success along with some examples.

Control Groups

The most credible approach for isolating the impact of an OD intervention is the use of control groups as in an experimental design process. This approach involves an experimental group that has the benefit of the intervention and a control group that does not have the intervention. The composition of both groups should be similar in characteristics and, if feasible, the selection of each group should be on a random basis. When this is possible, and both groups are subjected to the same environmental influences, the difference in the performance of the two groups can be attributed to the OD intervention. Figure 5-1 illustrates how the control group is set up. See the Case in Point sidebar for an example of using a control group in a leadership development program.

FIGURE 5-1. Use of Control Groups

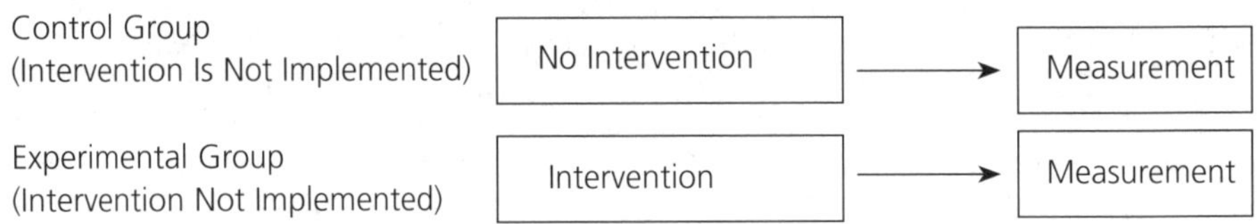

The use of control group arrangements has been around for a very long time. There is the story from biblical times in the book of Daniel, dating back to 600 B.C. that Daniel and his friends from Judah did not want to eat what the Babylonian royal court officials ate, so he proposed that he and his colleagues would eat vegetables and water for 10 days. When the 10 days were up, they compared Daniel's group to the group that ate the royal food and found a significant difference in energy and health.

One major disadvantage for control groups is withholding the intervention from one group. Neil Rackham describes a case where he used a control group, during which he observed a $6 million surplus in the group that went through his SPIN Selling program. When he presented the results, the CEO asked why the other group was kept from the benefit of the program. There needs to be a solid business reason for using a control group. If a control group is not an option, then consider the use of trend-line analysis.

Trend-Line Analysis

Another useful technique for approximating the impact of some OD interventions is trend-line analysis. In this approach, a trend line is drawn on a graph from a point that

Case in Point

The study focused on 500 managers who went through a major leadership development program. The participants' performance and business impact metrics were compared with that of a control group of an approximately equivalent number of managers with similar characteristics. Performance and business measures were tracked for the two groups for nine months in categories of 360-degree assessments, number of promotions, job satisfaction, number of legal complaints, turnover among direct reports, and turnover among the managers, themselves. The group who participated in the leadership development program had significantly more positive outcomes than the control group. Turnover and legal complaints were converted to monetary value, using internal standards for those values. The results showed a 25 percent ROI.

represents the beginning current performance level of the target audience, and extends to a point that represents the anticipated performance level without the OD intervention. Upon completion of the OD intervention, the actual performance is compared to the level the trend line predicted performance would be without the OD intervention. Any improvement of performance above what was predicted can be reasonably attributed to the OD intervention. While this is not an exact process, it provides a reasonable estimation of the impact of an OD intervention.

Figure 5-2 shows an example of trend-line analysis taken from an auto-parts manufacturer. The data are slightly exaggerated to illustrate the process. Voluntary turnover is presented before and after an OD intervention that was conducted in July. As shown in the figure, there was already a downward trend on the turnover rate prior to conducting the intervention. Although the intervention apparently had a dramatic effect on the reduction of voluntary turnover, the trend line shows that voluntary turnover would have continued, based on the trend that had been previously established. It is tempting to measure the improvement by comparing the average six-month voluntary turnover prior to the intervention to the average six months after the intervention. A more accurate comparison, however, is to use a six-month average after the intervention and compare it to the trend-line value at the midpoint of the six-month period after the intervention (April to January average turnover). In this example, the difference is 7 percent (33–26 = 7).

A primary disadvantage of this approach is that it is not necessarily accurate, although it may be as accurate as other methods described here. The use of this approach also assumes that the events that influenced the performance variable prior to the intervention are still in place after the intervention, except for the

FIGURE 5-2. Example of a Trend-Line Analysis

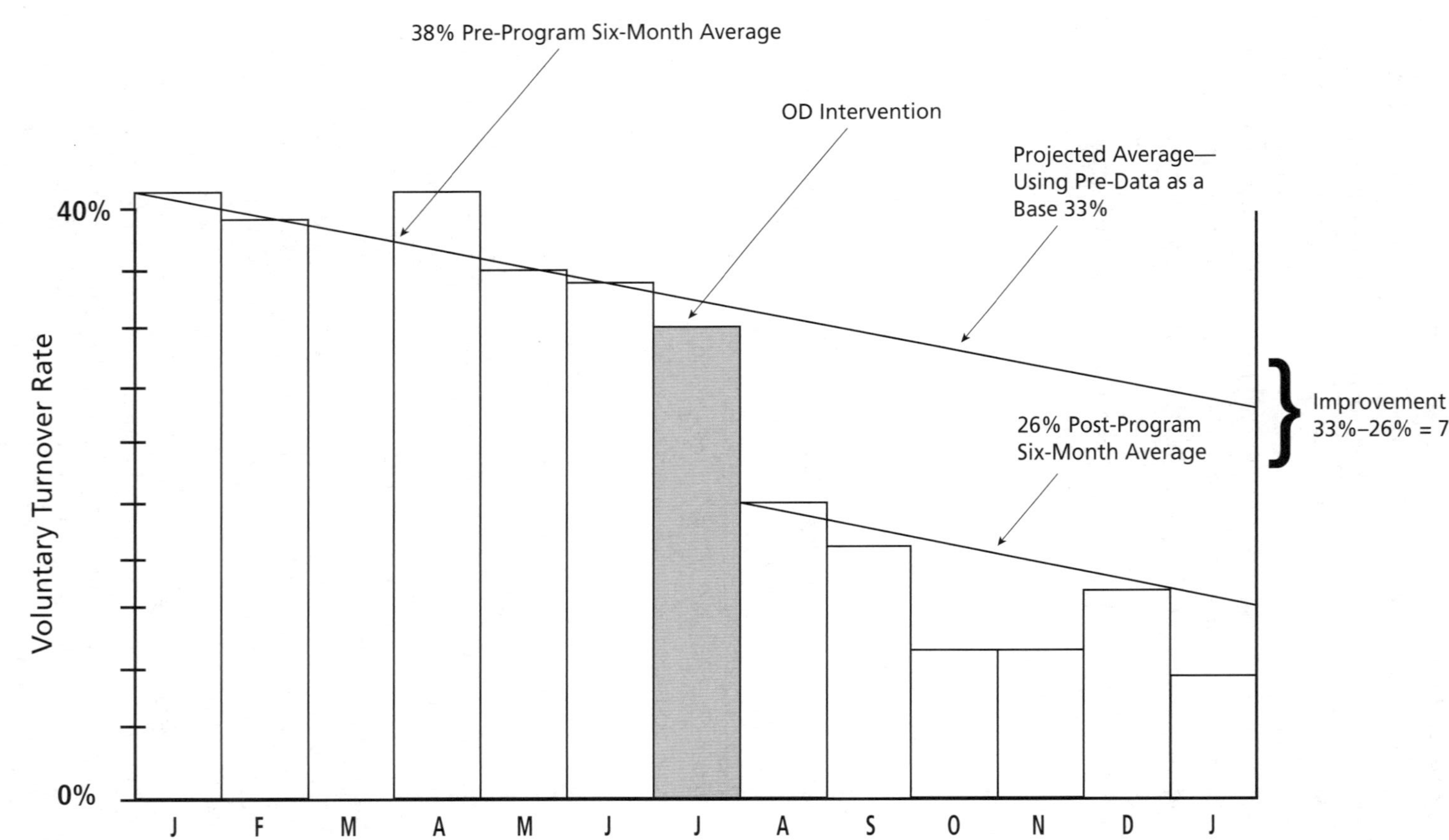

implementation of the OD intervention. Finally, this approach assumes that no new influences entered the situation. The trends that were established prior to the intervention will continue in the same relative direction. This may not always be the case.

The primary advantage of this approach is that it is simple, inexpensive, and takes very little effort. If historical data are available, a trend line can quickly be drawn and data estimated. While this process is not exact, it does provide a quick analysis of the intervention's impact.

Forecasting Methods

A more analytical approach to trend-line analysis is to use forecasting methods to predict the level of performance that might occur in the future if the OD intervention had not been undertaken. This approach represents a mathematical analysis of the trend-line analysis above. Instead of drawing a straight line, a linear equation is used to calculate a value of the anticipated performance improvement. A linear model is appropriate only when one other variable influenced the output performance, and that relationship can be characterized by a straight line. Figure 5-3 illustrates the relationship of variables used with forecasting.

The primary advantage of this process is that it can be an accurate predictor of the performance variables that would occur without implementing the intervention, if appropriate data and models are available. The method is simple for linear relationships. However, a major disadvantage to this approach occurs when many variables enter the process. The process becomes more complex and requires the use of sophisticated statistical analysis. Even then, the data may not fit the model. Unfortunately, many organizations have not developed mathematical relationships for output variables as a function of one or more inputs. Without them, the forecasting method is difficult to use. If the numbers are available, they could provide useful evidence of the impact of training. The presentation of specific methods is beyond the scope of this book and is contained in other works.

Participant Estimation

An easy method to isolate the impact of an OD intervention is to secure information directly from intervention participants. This approach assumes that participants are capable of determining or estimating how much of a performance improvement is related to the OD intervention. As the source of the performance, participants may have reliable input on the issue. Because their actions produced the change, they should have some estimation as to how much of the change was caused by the OD intervention. Although their input is an estimate, it will usually have considerable credibility with management groups because participants are at the center of the change or improvement resulting from the OD intervention.

FIGURE 5-3. Forecast Example

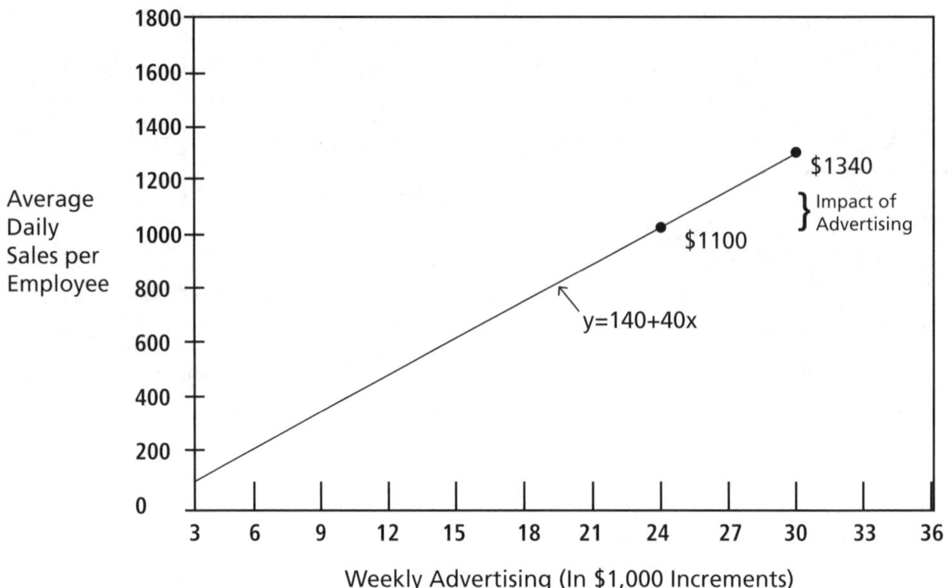

As an added enhancement to this method, management may be asked to approve the participants' estimates. For example, in an OD intervention involving a performance management system (performance appraisal and training), employees estimated the amount of savings attributed to the intervention. Table 5-1 shows a sample of these estimates. Managers at the next two levels above those participating reviewed and approved the estimates. So, in essence, the managers actually confirmed participants' estimates.

The process has some disadvantages. It is an estimate and, consequently, it does not have the accuracy desired by some HR and OD practitioners. Also, the input data may be unreliable because some individuals are uncomfortable with providing these types of estimates. Finally, some groups may be incapable of estimating improvements, even if they sincerely try. They might not be aware which factors exactly contributed to the results.

The approach has several advantages. It is a simple process and easily understood by participants and by others who review evaluation data. It is inexpensive, takes little time and analysis, and results in an efficient addition to the evaluation process. Although it is an estimate, it originates from a credible source: the individuals who actually produced the improvement.

TABLE 5-1. Example of a Team Member's Estimates

Factor That Influenced Improvement	% of Improvement Caused by	Confidence Expressed as a %	Adjusted % of Improvement Caused by
New Business Process	60%	80%	48%
Six Sigma	15%	70%	10.5%
Environmental Change	5%	60%	3%
System Change	20%	80%	16%
Other	__%	__%	__%
Total	**100%**		

Manager's Estimation

In some cases, upper management may estimate the percent of improvement attributed to the OD intervention. Although the process is subjective, the source of the estimate is a group that usually allocates funds and has a sense of what the value should be. With this approach, the source of these estimates is not usually based on direct knowledge of the process.

Case in Point

For example, Litton Guidance and Control Systems implemented a successful self-directed team process. Management identified other factors such as technology, procedures, and process changes that could have contributed to the improvement. Adjustments were made to account for these factors. After the other factors were considered, management then applied a subjective factor, in this case 60 percent, to represent the portion of the results that should be attributed to the OD intervention. The 60 percent factor was developed at a meeting with top executives and therefore had the benefit of group ownership. Applying this factor, the OD intervention took credit for 60 percent of the improvement in quality and productivity. While this process is subjective, the input or action comes from those who often provide the funds for the intervention. Sometimes their comfort level is what's most important. Because of the subjective nature of the process, this adjusted estimating process allows for a greater comfort level.

Customer Input

A helpful approach in some situations, such as an empowerment intervention, is to solicit input directly from customers concerning the impact of the intervention. In these situations, customers are asked to indicate their reasons for choosing a particular product or service, or to indicate how their reaction to the product or service organization has been influenced by individuals and their skills and abilities. This type of input focuses directly on what the OD intervention is often designed to improve. For example: Following a merger, one bank conducted a teller training intervention. Market research data showed that after training the percentage of customers who were dissatisfied with teller knowledge was reduced by 5 percent. (Training increased tellers' knowledge.) Therefore, 5 percent of the reduction of dissatisfied customers was directly attributable to the OD intervention.

Expert Estimation

Another approach to identifying factors that influence the impact of an OD program is to rely on external or internal experts to estimate what portion of results can be attributed to an OD intervention. With this process, the experts must be carefully selected based on their knowledge of the process, intervention, and situation. For example, an expert in quality might be able to provide estimates of how much quality improvement can be attributed to an OD intervention and what percent can be attributed to other factors. In another situation, an external expert can possibly estimate the extent to which improvement is made without the intervention. This amount is subtracted from the improvement, and it is assumed that the remainder can be attributed to the OD intervention. This approach appears to be most effective when the expert has been involved in similar interventions and estimates the impact of those factors based on previous experience or the use of historical data.

A potential variation on this approach may include using the external expert to produce the estimates from participants and supervisors and to then provide guidance on how to analyze and summarize the data. In some cases, it is helpful to have an expert actually facilitate the process with participants and supervisors. Experts, consultants, or researchers are usually available for almost any field in which there is training. They can bring their experience with similar situations into the analysis. This process has an advantage in that its credibility often reflects the reputation of the expert or independent consultant. Sometimes top management will place more confidence in external experts than in their own internal participants and supervisors.

CONVERTING DATA TO MONETARY UNITS

Chapter 4 presented the types of data collected for intervention evaluation. Before this data can be used to compare benefits with costs, it must be converted to monetary values. This section provides additional insight into practical ways to convert data to monetary values. Conversions of hard data (output, quality, cost, time) are discussed first, followed by soft data conversion.

Converting Increased Output

Changes in output are the goal of many OD interventions and in most situations the value of increased output can be easily calculated. For example, when implementing a sales incentive intervention, the change in output can easily be measured. The average sales before the intervention was installed are compared to the average sales after the intervention. It is calculated by multiplying the increase in sales by the average profit per sale. In another example, consider a packaging machine operator in a pharmaceutical plant. The operator packages drugs in boxes ready for shipment. Machine operators participate in an employee involvement intervention to learn how to increase production through better use of equipment and work procedures. The value of increased output is more difficult to pinpoint than the sales increase example. One approach is to calculate the unit labor cost of the packaging operation. Additional output of a unit ready for shipment saves the company the unit labor cost. Using this approach, the increase in output multiplied by the unit labor cost of packaging is the added value of the intervention. While this figure may not be exact because increases in output may affect the unit costs, it is usually accurate enough for measuring the return on an OD intervention.

Converting Direct Outputs

Converting cost savings to monetary values appears to be redundant. An OD intervention that produces a cost savings usually contributes an added value equal to the amount of the cost savings. However, the time value of money may slightly alter these values.

An amount of money at one point in time is worth more than the same amount at a later time. A simple discounted cash flow adjustment will place this comparison on an equal basis. Also, a cost savings generated by an employee or a group of employees over a long period might have a greater value than the actual savings, because costs normally increase during the period. This is best explained with an example. A group of employees operate a distribution center for publications. Supervisors have specific cost control responsibilities for their particular unit. They are held accountable for the direct variable costs and a portion of the fixed costs that are partially under their control. When costs seemed unusually high, the organization implemented cost control techniques as part of a continuous process improvement (CPI) intervention. Supervisors learned how to analyze costs and use the various reports to control costs. Both fixed and variable costs were monitored for a six-month period before and after the intervention to measure improvements. Part of these costs included equipment, wages, and supplies, all of which increased during the one-year period. To pinpoint an accurate value of the cost savings, the first six-month period costs were adjusted upward to what represented a cost target for comparison during the post-intervention period. Actual costs were compared with the target costs to determine the value of the cost savings as a result of the OD intervention, assuming no other factors influenced the cost savings.

Converting Time Savings

Many interventions are aimed at reducing the time to perform a task, deliver a service, or respond to a request. Time savings are important because employee time is money, in the form of wages, salaries, and benefits paid directly to the employee. The most common time savings results in reduced costs of effort involved in the OD intervention. The monetary savings are the hours saved multiplied by the effort cost per hour.

Improved Service

Another potential benefit of time savings is better service, particularly when production time, implementation time, construction time, or processing time is reduced so that the product or service is delivered to the client or customer in a shorter period of time. As a result, there is improved customer satisfaction, the value of which is difficult to quantify and will be discussed in the soft data section in this chapter. In some situations, reductions in time can avoid penalties. For example, with processing invoices in accounts payable, a reduction in processing time can avoid late payment penalties and possibly earn a discount. A reduction in time to complete a construction project can earn the company a sizable bonus.

Opportunity for Profit

A sometimes hidden, but potentially rewarding, benefit of time savings is the opportunity to make additional profit. For example, when a sales representative reduces the average time for a sales call, that representative has more time for sales calls. These additional calls should increase sales, which add to profits with little or no additional sales expense.

Converting Improved Quality

Quality improvement is an important and frequent target of OD interventions. Quality improvement interventions are developed to improve the quality of products, services, and processes. The cost of poor quality to an organization can be astounding. According to the late quality expert Phillip Crosby, an organization can probably increase its profits by 5 percent to 10 percent of sales if it concentrates on improving quality. To be effective, the measurable impact of a quality improvement intervention must be determined. To calculate the return on the intervention, the value of the quality improvement must be calculated. This value may have several components as described below.

Scrap/Waste

The most obvious cost of poor quality is the scrap or waste generated by mistakes. Defective products, spoiled raw materials, and discarded paperwork are the results of poor quality. This scrap and waste translates into a monetary value that can be used to calculate the impact of an improvement in quality. For example, in a production environment, the cost of a defective product can be easily calculated; it is the total cost incurred at the point the mistake is identified minus the salvage value. The costs of paper and computer entry errors can be significant. For example, the cost of an error on a purchase order can be enormous if the wrong items are ordered.

Rework

Many mistakes and errors result in costly rework to correct the mistake. The most costly reworks occur when a product is delivered to a customer but must be returned for correction, or when an expensive intervention is implemented with serious errors. In determining the cost of rework, labor and direct cost are both significant. Maintaining a staff to perform rework is an additional overhead cost for the organization. In a manufacturing plant, the cost of rework is in the range of 15 to 70 percent of a plant's productivity. In banks, an estimated 35 percent of operating costs could be blamed on correcting errors.

Customer/Client Dissatisfaction

Customer and client dissatisfaction represents a tremendous loss for the organization when errors and mistakes are made. Among customers who complain, more than one-half will do business with an organization after the complaint is resolved. If the customer perceives his complaints were resolved quickly, this number spikes to 95 percent. In some cases, serious mistakes can result in lost business. Customer dissatisfaction is difficult to quantify, and attempts to arrive at a monetary value may be impossible. Usually, the judgment and expertise of sales and marketing management are the best sources for estimating the cost of a dissatisfied customer. It may be more realistic to list an improvement in customer satisfaction as an advantage of improved quality without trying to quantify it.

However, experts in service quality insist that customer and client dissatisfaction can be measured. Some refer to this as measuring the market damage of poor service quality. One approach is to survey customers who have had good and bad experiences and ask them whether they are likely to do business with that particular company again. Later, the same people can be surveyed to find out whether they did do business with the company. Then researchers use a formula to measure the monetary damage bad service did to repeat business.

Costs of Quality

The quality problem is extensive, and various components affect the cost of poor quality. These components are sometimes grouped and often referred to categorically as preventive costs, appraisal costs, and failure costs. Crosby contends that total expenditures for these items should be no more than 2.5 percent of sales. Although it may seem challenging to calculate the numbers, some consultants and practitioners are able to make this calculation using surveys. This process requires employees to estimate how much time they spend doing work that falls into each of the three categories above. The figure is then multiplied by the standard labor wage rate and adjusted with a benefits factor. An American-based insurance company uses a survey process to estimate this cost. Each team lists the amount of time each member devotes to each category in an average week as well as the specific costs incurred by variations from quality standards. The numbers were not precise, but the estimates resulted in a total figure of 44 percent of overhead. The result was consistent among the divisions. This measure provided an indication of the magnitude of the problem and served as a source of ideas for the team throughout the year. It also served as a benchmark by which to measure the team in years to come.

Converting Soft Data

While soft data are not as desirable as hard data, they are important in OD measurement and evaluation. The difficulty with soft data often arises in assigning monetary values to the data. Most assignments of value are subjective and must be used with some caution. Several approaches are available to convert the soft data to a monetary value and are presented below.

Historical Costs

Occasionally an organization will develop and accumulate cost for specific soft data items. For example, some organizations monitor the cost of grievances. Although an extremely variable item, the average cost per grievance provides a basis for estimating the cost savings for a reduction in grievances. Because of their relative accuracy, historical costs, if available, should always be used to estimate the value of soft data items.

Expert Opinion

Expert opinions, either internal or external, are sometimes used to estimate the value of soft data improvements. Internal experts are those employees who are proficient and knowledgeable in their fields. For example, a purchasing expert may estimate the salvage value of defective parts, an industrial engineer might estimate the time that it takes to complete a task or perform a function, and a marketing analyst might estimate the cost of a dissatisfied customer. Using internal experts provides excellent opportunities to recognize individuals in the organization. Chances are, their expert analysis will not be challenged because others in the organization have no better basis to make the estimate. External experts may also provide an estimate, depending on their expertise in a given field. One consultant, for example, estimated the cost of work slowdowns and was able to use the figure with several organizations by providing an expert opinion.

External Studies

Extensive analyses of similar data in other organizations may be extrapolated to fit an internal situation. For example, many experts have attempted to calculate the cost of absenteeism. Although these estimates can vary considerably, they may serve as a rough estimate for other calculations with some adjustments for the specific organization. There are literally hundreds of studies conducted in the literature covering the cost of variables such as absenteeism, turnover, tardiness, grievances, complaints, and loss of time due to accidents. Typical sources to pursue may include Corporate Leadership Council, *Academy of Management Journal*, *Journal of Applied Psychology*, *Personnel Psychology*, *Human Resources Management Review*, *OD Practitioner*, *Human Resource Development Quarterly*, and *Personnel Journal*.

Practitioners rarely venture into external studies probably because there is not enough dialogue between the OD researchers and the practitioners. Each group seems to have a misunderstanding of the other's role, and they only mesh at times when it is convenient for both. Practitioners should learn more about research studies and publications and possibly influence future research.

Participant Estimation

Employees directly involved in an OD intervention may be capable of estimating the value of an improvement. Either during the intervention or in a follow-up, participants should be asked to estimate the value of the improvements. To provide further insight, participants should also be asked to furnish the basis for their estimate and their level of confidence in it. Estimations by participants are credible and may be more realistic than other sources because participants are usually directly involved with the improvement and are knowledgeable of the issues. If provided encouragement and examples, participants are often creative at estimating these values. For example, in one organization, in response to a special OD intervention, staff managers were asked to estimate the value of reducing the time to recruit a new employee. Although their responses were not precise, they provided a credible estimate of this value from the customers of the recruiting section.

Management Estimation

A final strategy for converting soft data to monetary values is to ask managers who are concerned about the intervention's evaluation to estimate the value of an improvement. Several management groups may be targets for this estimation including supervisors of intervention participants, middle management, or even the C-Suite.

In summary, these strategies are effective for converting soft data to monetary values when calculating a return on an OD intervention. One word of caution is in order. Whenever a monetary value is assigned to subjective information, it needs to be fully explained to the audience receiving the information. When there is a range of possible values, the most conservative one should be used to ensure credibility for the process.

CALCULATING THE RETURN

The return on investment is an intriguing and important calculation for the OD practitioner. Yet, it is a figure that must be used with caution and care because it can be interpreted or misinterpreted in many ways. This section presents some general guidelines to help calculate the return and interpret its meaning.

Defining the Return on Investment

The term *return on investment* (ROI) may appear to be out of place in OD. The expression originates from finance and accounting and usually refers to the pretax contribution measured against controllable assets. It measures the anticipated profitability of an investment and is used as a standard measure of the performance of divisions and profit centers within a business.

In many situations, a group of employees is involved in an OD intervention at one time, so the investment figure should be the total costs of analysis, development, implementation, operating, and evaluation lumped together for the denominator of the equation. With these considerations, for calculating the return on investment in OD, the following formula is used:

$$\text{ROI} = \frac{\text{Net Benefits}}{\text{Intervention Costs}} \times 100$$

The formula is multiplied by 100 to convert it to a percent. To keep calculations simple the return should be based on pretax conditions and avoid issues such as investment tax credits, depreciation, tax shields, and other related items. The total intervention costs are all related costs including analysis, development, implementation, operating, and evaluation. The net benefits could result from cost savings, additional revenues, or improvements. They are not limited to any particular type of benefit, but are converted to a monetary value. It is recommended that annual benefit be used in the formula.

To illustrate this calculation, consider an OD intervention designed to reduce error rates. Because of the intervention, the average daily error rate per employee dropped from 20 to 15. Before the intervention, employees spent an average of two hours correcting errors. If employees average $20.00 per hour and 20 employees completed the intervention, the weekly operational savings for this intervention using base pay savings only is $1,000. The annual savings is $52,000. If the OD intervention costs $40,000, the return on investment after the first month is:

$$ROI = \frac{\$52,000 - \$40,000}{\$40,000} \times 100 = 30\%$$

ROI is usually useful for evaluating expenditures relating to an OD intervention. Although the term is common and conveys an adequate meaning of financial evaluation, the finance and accounting staff may take issue with calculations involving the return on investment for an OD intervention. Because of this, some OD professionals suggest that a more appropriate label would be return on human resources. Others avoid the word "return" and just calculate the monetary savings as a result of the intervention, which is basically subtracting the costs from the benefits. These figures may be more meaningful to managers who use ROI calculations for capital expenditures. ROI may be calculated prior to an OD intervention to estimate the potential cost effectiveness or after an intervention to measure the results achieved. The methods of calculation are the same. However, the estimated return before an intervention is usually calculated for a proposal to implement the intervention. The data for its calculation are more subjective and usually less reliable than the data from an intervention completion. Because of this factor, management may require a higher ROI for an OD intervention in the proposal stage.

Additional Methods for Evaluating Investments

Because of the limitations with ROI, other approaches for evaluating OD investments should be explored. Several methods are available that reflect efficiency in the use of invested funds. The most common approaches are described next.

Payback Period

A payback period is a common method for evaluating a major expenditure. With this approach, the annual cash proceeds (savings) produced by investment are equated to the original cash outlay required by the investment to arrive at some multiple of cash proceeds equal to the original investment. Measurement is usually in terms of years and months. If the cost savings generated from an OD intervention is constant each year, the payback period is determined by dividing the total original cash investment (development costs, outside intervention purchase, and so on) by the amount of the expected annual savings. The savings represent the net savings after the intervention expenses are subtracted.

For example, if the intervention costs are $100,000, with a three-year useful life, and the annual net savings from the intervention is expected to be $40,000, then:

$$\text{Payback Period} = \frac{\text{Intervention Costs}}{\text{Annual Net Savings}}$$

The intervention will "pay back" the original investment in two and a half years. The payback period is simple to use but has the limitation of ignoring the time value of money.

Benefit-Cost Ratio

Another method for evaluating the investment in OD is the benefit-cost ratio. Similar to the ROI, this ratio consists of the total of the benefits derived from the program expressed in monetary units, divided by the total cost of the intervention. A benefit-cost ratio greater than 1 indicates a positive return. A ratio of less than 1 indicates a loss. The benefits portion of the ratio is a tabulation of all the benefits derived from the intervention converted to monetary values as described earlier in this chapter. The total costs include all the cost categories as described earlier. The ratio has been used to evaluate projects, particularly in the public sector, beginning in the 1900s. Since then, it has been used for project evaluation in many different settings.

Benefit-cost ratio is often used because it is not usually connected with standard accounting procedures. Although the benefits are converted to monetary values, steering away from the standard accounting measures is a more comfortable approach. Sometimes there is a feeling that the accounting measures communicate a preciseness that is not always available when calculating the benefits or the cost portion of the equation.

Consequences of Not Providing an Intervention

A final method for calculating the return on OD that has received recent attention is the consequences of not implementing an OD intervention. An organization's inability to perform adequately might mean that it is unable to take on additional business or that it may be losing existing business because of an untrained, unmotivated, underpaid, or disruptive workforce. This approach, at least intuitively, provides the basis for many preventive interventions such as safety and health, affirmative action litigation prevention, and labor management cooperation efforts. This method involves:

- Establishing the existence of an actual or potential loss.
- Obtaining an estimate of the worth of the business in actual or potential value and if possible, the OD intervention's value to the organization in terms of profit.
- Isolating the factors involved in a lack of performance that may create the loss of business or the inability to take on additional business. This includes lack of staff, lack of training, inability to staff quickly, inadequate facilities in which to expand, inadequate equipment, and excessive turnover. If there is more than one factor involved, determine the impact of each factor on the loss of income.
- Estimating the total cost of OD using the techniques outlined in an earlier chapter and comparing costs with benefits. This approach has some disadvantages. The potential loss of income can be highly subjective and difficult to measure. Also it may be difficult to isolate the factors involved and to determine their weight relative to lost income.

COSTS OF THE INTERVENTION

Diagnosis yields a need, and then the organization designs and develops a solution or acquires one and implements it. The OD team routinely reports to the client or sponsor throughout the process and then undertakes an evaluation to show the project's success. A group of costs also supports the process (e.g., administrative support and overhead costs). For costs to be fully understood, the project needs to be analyzed in these different categories.

The most important task is to define which specific costs are included in a tabulation of program costs. This step involves decisions that will be made by the OD team and, in most cases, approved by management. If appropriate, finance and accounting staff may need to approve the list. Table 5-1 shows the recommended cost categories for a fully loaded, conservative approach to estimating costs. Each category is described next.

Diagnostics/Needs Assessment Costs

One of the most overlooked cost items is the cost of conducting the initial assessment or diagnosis of the need for the OD project. In some projects, this cost is zero because the project is implemented without an initial assessment of need. However, as organizations focus increased attention on needs assessment, this item will become a more significant cost in the future.

While it's best to collect data on all costs associated with the assessment and diagnosis to the fullest extent possible, estimates are appropriate. These costs include the time of OD team members to conduct the assessment, direct fees, expenses for external consultants who conduct the diagnosis, and internal services and supplies used in the analysis. The total costs are usually prorated over the life of the project. Depending on the type and nature of the project, the life cycle should be kept to a reasonable number in the one- to two-year time frame. The exception would be for expensive projects for which the needs are not expected to change significantly for several years.

Design and Development Costs

One of the most significant items is the cost of developing the intervention. This cost item includes internal staff and consultant time for development of software, CD-ROMs, job aids, and other support material directly related to the project. As with diagnostics costs, development costs are usually prorated, perhaps by using the same time frame. Three to five years is recommended unless the project is expected to remain unchanged for many years and the development costs are significant.

Acquisition Costs

In lieu of development costs, many organizations purchase software or programs to use off-the-shelf or in a modified format. The acquisition costs for these programs include the purchase price and other costs associated with the rights to implement the program. These acquisition costs should be prorated typically over three or five years using the same rationale described above. If the organization needs to modify or further develop the program, those costs should be included as development costs. In practice, many programs have both acquisition costs and development costs.

Implementation Costs

Perhaps the most important segment of LD costs is implementation. Five major categories are included:

- **Salaries of coordinators and organizers.** The salaries of all individuals involved in coordination and direct support should be included. If a coordinator is involved in more than one program, the time should be allocated to the specific program under review. The key point is to account for all the direct time of internal employees or external consultants who work with the program. Include the employee benefits factor each time direct labor costs are involved.

- **Materials and supplies.** Specific project materials such as workbooks, handouts, brochures, guides, job aids, and CD-ROMs should be included in the delivery costs, along with license fees, user fees, and royalty payments.
- **Travel expenses.** Include direct costs of travel, if required, for participants, facilitators, and coordinators. Lodging, meals, and other expenses also fall under this category.
- **Facilities for sessions.** Take into account the direct cost of the meeting facilities. When external meetings are held, this item represents the direct charge from the conference center or hotel. If meetings are held internally, use of the meeting room represents a cost to the organization and should be included, even if it is not the practice to include facility costs in other cost reporting.
- **Participating group members' salaries and benefits.** The salaries plus employee benefits of group members for their time away from work represent an expense that should be included. Estimates are appropriate in the analysis.

Operation and Maintenance

This item includes all costs related to routine operation of the program. The category encompasses all costs in the same categories listed under implementation, plus perhaps equipment and services.

Evaluation

The evaluation cost is included in the program costs to compute the fully loaded cost. For an ROI evaluation, the costs include developing the evaluation strategy and plans, designing instruments, collecting data, analyzing data, and preparing and presenting results. Cost categories include time, purchased services, materials, purchased instruments, and surveys.

Overhead

A final charge is the cost of overhead: the additional costs of the OD function not directly charged to a particular program. The overhead category represents any OD function cost not considered in the previous calculations. Typical items include the cost of administrative support, administrative expenses, salaries of OD managers, and other fixed costs. A rough estimate developed through some type of allocation plan is usually sufficient.

Intangibles

Perhaps the first step to understanding intangibles is to clearly define the difference between tangible and intangible assets in a business organization. As shown in Table 5-2, tangible assets are required for business operations; they are readily visible, rigorously quantified, and routinely represented as line items on balance sheets. Intangible assets are the key to competitive advantage. They are invisible, difficult to quantify, and not tracked through traditional accounting practices. With this distinction, it is easy to understand why intangible measures are more challenging to convert to money. In this next section, we will highlight a handful of intangible measures that are relevant for OD.

TABLE 5-2. Comparison of Tangible and Intangible Assets

Tangible Assets (Required for Business Operations)	Intangible Assets (Key to Competitive Advantage in Knowledge)
Readily visible	Invisible
Rigorously quantified	Difficult to quantify
Part of the balance sheet	Not tracked through accounting practices
Investment produces known returns	Assessment based on assumptions
Can be easily duplicated	Cannot be bought or imitated
Depreciates with use	Appreciates with purposeful use
Has finite application	Multi-application without reducing value
Best managed with "scarcity" mentality	Best managed with "abundance" mentality
Best leveraged through control	Best leveraged through alignment
Can be accumulated	Dynamic: short shelf life when not in use

Organizational Commitment/Employee Engagement

In recent years, organizational commitment (OC) measures have complemented or replaced job satisfaction measures. Organizational commitment measures go beyond employee satisfaction and include the extent to which the employees identify with organizational goals, mission, philosophy, value, policies, and practices. In recent years, the concept of involvement and engagement with the organization has become a key issue. Employee engagement (EE) is now the preferred measure. Employee engagement measures the extent to which employees are actively engaged in decisions and issues on the job. Organizational commitment and employee engagement measures closely correlate with productivity and other performance improvement measures, in contrast to employee satisfaction, which does not always correlate with improvements in productivity. As OC/EE scores improve (according to a standard index), a corresponding improvement in productivity should develop. The organizational commitment/employee engagement is often measured the same way that attitude surveys are, with a 5- or 7-point scale taken directly from employees or groups of employees. Productivity is usually measured by revenue per employee.

Organizational commitment, or employee engagement, is rarely converted to monetary value. Although some relationships have been developed to link it to more tangible data, this research is still in development. For most studies, they would be listed as intangibles.

Culture and Climate

Organization culture is a very important factor for the OD practitioner's work. Various OD culture change projects attempt to strengthen, solidify, or adjust the culture. The culture in some organizations is distinct and defined, but it can be a challenge to measure precisely.

Some organizations use culture instruments to collect data on this measure before and after a program to measure improvement. The scores on these instruments represent important data that may be connected directly to the intervention. In practice, it is challenging to convert culture data to monetary value; therefore, culture change is sometimes listed as an intangible measure.

Some organizations conduct climate surveys, which reflect work climate changes such as communication, openness, trust, and quality of feedback. Closely related to organizational commitment and culture, climate surveys are very general and often focus on a range of workplace issues and environmental enablers and inhibitors. Climate surveys conducted before and after an OD intervention is implemented may reflect the extent to which the intervention has changed these measures.

Diversity

Diversity continues to be important as organizations strive to develop and nurture a diverse workforce. Organizational initiatives influence the diversity mix of the organization, and various data are available to measure the impact of focusing on diversity. The diversity mix is a measure showing employee categories along diversity definitions such as race, creed, color, national origin, age, religion, and sex. This diversity mix shows the makeup of the team at any given time and is not a measure that can be converted to monetary value credibly.

The payoff of having a diverse group influences several other measures, including absenteeism, turnover, discrimination complaints, morale, and sometimes productivity and quality. Also, many diversity perception instruments are available to measure the attitudes of employees toward diversity issues; they are often administered before and after diversity projects. In addition, some organizations collect input on diversity issues in an annual feedback survey. All of these measures are important and reveal progress on an important issue, but that is difficult to convert directly to monetary value and are usually listed as intangibles.

Stress Reduction

OD initiatives can reduce work-related stress by preparing employees to identify and confront stress factors to improve job performance, accomplish more in a workday, and relieve tension and anxiety. The subsequent reduction in stress may be directly linked to the intervention. Although excessive stress may be directly linked to other, easy-to-convert data, such as productivity, absenteeism, and medical claims, it is usually listed as an intangible benefit that is difficult to convert to monetary values.

FINAL THOUGHTS

This chapter discussed four key issues in calculating the OD contribution. The first and one of the most critical is the concept of isolating the OD intervention, which determines the extent to which the improvement was caused by the OD intervention. The second issue involves converting data to monetary values. Regardless of the type of data, there are a number of strategies that can be extremely helpful in translating the data to monetary values to use in ROI formulas. Calculating the return on investment, a third factor of data analysis, is straightforward; however, there are several credible methods to calculate the return. While not appropriate for every intervention, it is desirable in some situations and should be used in the analysis of those situations. The organization should determine which types of interventions will ultimately command a return on investment calculation and then set goals to meet their targets. The fourth aspect is the cost of the intervention, and finally, the intangibles close out this section on data analysis. Data collection and analysis have little use without conveying the results to the right audience in the right way. In the next chapter, we will highlight how to communicate the results.

6

Communicating Results

Think like a wise man but communicate in the language of the people.

—William Butler Yeats

An OD group from a large telecommunications organization conducted an evaluation of an OD project. The project was to improve quality and speed of service through reorganization and leadership development. Once the project was concluded, the OD team measured the results. The project results were a mixed bag. The quality of service had improved but the speed of service had not; in fact, it was slower than before. To share their findings, the OD team tried to get on the executive calendar to share results in person; the meeting was to take place six weeks later. Knowing that there were findings that needed to be communicated immediately, the OD team generated a report, which included major findings and charts and graphs, and distributed to the executive team via email. Unfortunately, the report was overlooked in the sea of emails received by the executive team. It wasn't till the face-to-face meeting that the executive team saw the mixed results, and with a lot of questions raised, the tone of the meeting was tense and uncomfortable. The OD team leader remarked to her team afterward, *"If I had to do it again, I would have escalated the need to communicate these findings in a different way."*

The issues raised by this scenario represent common challenges of communicating findings. And having worked in hundreds of organizations working on evaluation (with our combined experience), we have seen a wide variety of challenges in communicating results. Everything from reports with personal agendas to dealing with stakeholders who don't know their data and evaluation needs to groups who seemingly hide their findings under a rock. This real example helps to illustrate the nature and challenge of communication and evaluation in today's workplace.

What and when is the best way to convey results? What is the purpose for the communication? Who is the intended audience? This chapter is about our final step in the ROI process, and will address these questions and more. This chapter will highlight the dos and don'ts of communicating evaluation findings, describe a best practice report formula that can be repeatedly used to sustain momentum and change, and outline key ingredients for a communication plan.

THE DOS OF COMMUNICATING RESULTS

Do Communicate Timely

Usually, project results should be communicated as soon as they are known and are packaged for presentation. As in our opening story, the timing of the results was a critical factor in the project. Not sharing the results in a timely fashion can lead to a missed opportunity for well-timed improvement. Several questions about timing must be addressed:

- Is the audience prepared for the information, when considering the content and other events?
- Are they expecting it?
- When is the best time to have the maximum impact on the audience?

Do Gear Your Communication to a Specific Audience

The communication will be more efficient when it is designed for a specific group. The message can be specifically tailored to the interests, needs, and expectations of the group. The length, content, detail, and slant will vary with the audience. Table 6-1 shows the specific audience groups with the most common reasons for communicating results.

Table 6-1. Common Target Audiences

Primary Target Audience	Reason for Communication
Client, top executives	To secure approval for the project
Immediate managers	To gain support for the project
Team members, team leaders	To secure agreement with the issues, to create the desire for a team member to be involved, and to improve the results and quality of future feedback
Top executives	To enhance the credibility of the project
Immediate managers	To reinforce the processes
OD team	To drive action for improvement
Team leaders	To prepare participants for the project
Stakeholders	To show the complete results of the project
Client, project team	To underscore the importance of measuring results
All employees	To demonstrate accountability for expenditures
Prospective clients	To market future projects

Probably the most important target audience is the client and often, this involves senior management. They need information to approve funding. The entire management group may also need to be informed about project results in a general way.

Management's support for, and involvement in, the OD process is important to the success of the effort. The department's credibility is another key issue. Communicating project results to management can help establish this credibility.

The importance of communicating with a group member's supervisor is probably obvious. In some cases, supervisors need to support and allow employees to be involved in OD projects. An adequate return on investment in OD projects improves their commitment to the OD function, as well as enhances OD's credibility with them.

Group members themselves need feedback on the overall success of their efforts. This target audience is often overlooked under the assumption that group members do not need to know about the overall success of the program.

OD team members should receive information about program results, and depending on how an OD team is set up in terms of reporting relationships, perhaps include HR as well. For small teams, the individual conducting the evaluation may be the same person who coordinated the effort. For larger departments, evaluation may be a separate function. In either case, the team needs detailed information on the project's effectiveness so that adjustments can be made if the project is to be repeated.

Do Carefully Select Your Mode of Communication

For a specific group, one medium may be more effective than others. Face-to-face meetings may be better with some groups than special reports. A brief summary to senior management will more than likely be more effective than a full-blown evaluation report. The selection of an appropriate medium will help improve the effectiveness of the process. Table 6-2 illustrates options for communicating results.

Table 6-2. Options for Communicating Results

Detailed Reports	Brief Reports	Electronic Reporting	Mass Publications
Impact study	Executive summary	Website	Announcements
Case study (internal)	Slide overview	Email	Bulletins
Case study (external)	One-page summary	Blog	Newsletters
Major articles	Brochure	Video	Brief articles

Do Remain Neutral in Your Communication

The challenge for the evaluator is to remain neutral and unbiased. Let the results inform as to whether the OD efforts hit the mark. Facts are separated from fiction, and data-driven statements replace opinions. Some target audiences may view communication from the OD department with skepticism and may look for biased information and opinions. Boastful statements will sometimes turn off individuals, and most of the content of the communication will be lost. Observable, believable facts carry more weight than extreme claims.

Do Include Testimonials in Your Report

Testimonials are more effective if they are from individuals with audience credibility. Attitudes are strongly influenced by others, particularly by those who are admired or respected. Testimonials about OD project results, when solicited from individuals who are generally respected in the organization, can have a strong impact on the effectiveness of the message. One organization, when implementing a new customer interface intervention included testimonials from key customers in their report out. This was received extremely well by the executive team.

Do Be Consistent in the Way You Communicate

Look for ways to include evaluation reporting, using the timing and forums of other organization reports. The content of the communication should be consistent with organization practices. A special communication at an unusual time may create more work than it's worth. When a particular group, such as senior management, regularly receives communication, the information should continue even if the results are not what were desired. If selected results are omitted, it might leave the impression that only good results are reported.

Do Drive Improvement From Your Communication

Information is collected at different points during the process, and providing feedback to involved groups enables them to take action and make adjustments if needed. Thus, the quality and timeliness of communication are critical to making improvements. Even after the project is completed, communication is necessary to make sure the target audience fully understands the results achieved, and how the results may be enhanced in future projects or in the current project, if it is still operational. Communication is the key to making important adjustments at all phases of the project.

THE DON'TS OF COMMUNICATING RESULTS

Don't Hide Your Results

The least desired communication action is doing nothing. Communicating results is almost as important as producing results. Getting results without communicating them is like not calling the person who invited you for dinner to cancel because you ran out of gas. By not sharing the findings from your project, the organization can miss out on a key opportunity to make adjustments and bring about the change that is desired.

Don't Overlook the Potentially Political Charged Implications of Communication

Communication is one of those issues that can cause major problems. Because the results of a project may be closely linked to political issues within an organization, communicating the results can upset some individuals while pleasing others. If certain individuals do not receive the information, or if it is delivered inconsistently between groups, problems can quickly surface. Not only must the information be understood, but issues relating to fairness, quality, and political correctness make it crucial that the communication be constructed and delivered effectively to all key individuals.

Don't Skimp on the Recommendations Section of Your Final Report

This is probably one of the most critical sections of the final report and yet, it seems it is often a last minute thought or skipped altogether. In the report-writing world, recommendations are the main conduit to change happening. The best recommendations include specific action-oriented steps that come from the conclusions of the evaluation study and then are discussed with key stakeholders for buy-in and ownership. The point is to collaborate with stakeholders on this section so that the results and the action that is needed are internalized.

Don't Exclude the Audience's Opinion

Opinions are difficult to change, and a negative opinion toward a project or a team may not change with the mere presentation of facts. However, the presentation of facts alone may strengthen the opinions held by those who already support the project. Presentation of the results reinforces their position and provides them with a defense in discussions with others. A project team with a high level of credibility and respect may have a relatively easy time communicating results. Low credibility can create problems when one is trying to be persuasive.

THE REPORT FORMULA

The type of report to be issued depends on the degree of detail in the information presented to the various target audiences. Brief summaries of project results with appropriate charts may be sufficient for some communication efforts. In other situations, particularly those involving major projects requiring extensive funding, a detailed evaluation report is crucial. A complete and comprehensive impact study report is usually necessary. This report can then be used as the basis for more streamlined information aimed at specific audiences and using various media. The report formula outlined below is one we use repeatedly to convey results in an effective manner. We have found it has all of the necessary ingredients to communicate outcomes in the best possible way.

- General Information
  - Background: Why was this intervention selected? What were the needs that precipitated the solution?
  - Objectives of study: What are the goals and targets for this project? What are the intended results?
- Methodology for Impact Study
  - Levels of evaluation: Describe the evaluation framework to set the state for showing the results.
  - ROI Process: Describe the 10-step process that was used.
  - Collecting data: What methods were selected to collect data and why? Also, when were data collected?
  - Isolating the effects of the projects: What method was used to isolate the effects of the intervention and why?
  - Converting data to monetary values: What method was used to convert data to money?
- Data Analysis: How were data analyzed? What methods were used?
- Costs: Itemize the costs of the intervention.
- Results: General Information
  - Response profile: Include demographics of the population that responded or participated in the evaluation. If a questionnaire was used, what was the return rate and the anticipated return rate?
- Results: Reaction and Satisfaction
  - Data sources
  - Data summary
  - Key issues
- Results: Learning
  - Data sources
  - Data summary
  - Key issues
- Results: Application and Implementation
  - Data sources
  - Data summary
  - Key issues
- Results: Impact and Consequences
  - Data sources
  - Data summary
  - Key issues

- Results: ROI
- Results: Intangible Measures
- Barriers and Enablers: This section of the report can be a powerful mechanism to lead into conclusions and recommendations. What obstacles were experienced that kept the organization from experiencing the kind of results they wanted? If there were barriers noted, then this should turn into some action items for the organization.
- Conclusions: Summarize key findings from the data.
- Recommendations: Based on the conclusions, what type of action needs to take place? What are stakeholders willing to do?

While the impact study report is an effective, professional way to present ROI data, several cautions are in order. Since this report documents the success of a project involving a large group of employees, credit for the success must go completely to those involved, the organization members who participated in the project and their immediate leaders. Their performance generated the success.

The methodology should be clearly explained, along with the assumptions made in the analysis. The reader should easily see how the values were developed and how specific steps were followed to make the process more conservative, credible, and accurate. Detailed statistical analyses should be placed in an appendix.

Meetings

If used properly, meetings are fertile ground for the communication of project results. All organizations hold a variety of meetings, and some may provide the proper context to convey project results. Along the chain of command, staff meetings are held to review progress, discuss current problems, and distribute information. These meetings can be an excellent forum for discussing the results achieved in a project that relates to the group's activities. Project results can be sent to executives for use in a staff meeting, or a member of the project team can attend the meeting to make the presentation.

Regular meetings with management groups are a common practice. Typically, discussions will focus on items that might be of help to work units. The discussion of a project and its results can be integrated into the regular meeting format. A few organizations have initiated the use of periodic meetings for all key stakeholders, where the project leader reviews progress and discusses next steps. A few highlights from interim project results can be helpful in building interest, commitment, and support for the project.

Presentation of Results to Senior Management

Perhaps one of the most challenging and stressful types of communication is presenting an impact study to the senior management team, which also serves as the client for a project. The challenge is convincing this highly skeptical and critical group that outstanding results have been achieved (assuming they have) in a very reasonable time frame, addressing the salient points, and making sure the managers understand the process. Two potential reactions can create problems. First, if the results are very impressive, making the managers accept the data may be difficult. On the other extreme, if the data are negative, ensuring that managers don't overreact to the results and look for someone to blame is important. Several guidelines can help ensure that this process is planned and executed properly.

Arrange a face-to-face meeting with senior team members to review the first one or two major impact studies. If they are unfamiliar with the ROI Methodology, such a meeting is necessary to make sure they understand the process. The good news is that they will probably attend the meeting because they have never seen ROI data developed for this type of project. The bad news is that it takes a lot of time, usually about an hour, for this presentation. After the meeting with a couple of presentations, an executive summary may suffice. At this point, the senior members will understand the process, so a shortened version may be appropriate. The famous saying by Pythagoras is relevant here: *Do not say a little in many words but a great deal in a few*. Once the target audience is familiar with the process, a brief version may be developed, including a one- to two-page summary with charts and graphs showing the six types of measures.

The results should not be disseminated before the initial presentation or even during the session, but should be saved until the end of the session. This will allow enough time to present the process and gather reactions to it before the target audience sees the ROI calculation. Present the ROI Methodology step by step:

- showing how the data were collected
- when they were collected
- who provided them
- how the effect of the project was isolated from other influences
- how data were converted to monetary values.

The various assumptions, adjustments, and conservative approaches are presented along with the total cost of the project, so that the target audience will begin to buy into the process of developing the ROI.

When the data are actually presented, the results are given one level at a time, starting with Level 1, moving through Level 5, and ending with the intangibles. This allows the audience to observe the reaction, learning, application and implementation, business impact, and ROI procedures. After some discussion of the meaning of the ROI, the intangible measures are presented. Allocate time for each level as appropriate for the audience. This helps to defuse potential emotional reactions to a very positive or negative ROI.

Show the consequences of additional accuracy if this is an issue. The trade-off for more accuracy and validity often is more expense. Address this issue when necessary, agreeing to add more data if they are required. Collect concerns and reaction involving the process and make adjustments accordingly for the next presentation. Collectively, these steps will help in the preparation and presentation of one of the most important meetings in the ROI process.

Routine Communication Tools

To reach a wide audience, the OD practitioner can use internal, routine publications. Whether a newsletter, magazine, newspaper, or electronic file, these media usually reach all employees or stakeholders. The content can have a significant impact if communicated appropriately. The scope should be limited to general-interest articles, announcements, and interviews.

Results communicated through these types of media must be important enough to arouse general interest. For example, a story with the headline "New Software and Business Process Helps Twice as Many Products" will catch the attention of many readers because it is likely they participated in the project and can appreciate the relevance of the results. Reports on the accomplishments of a group of organization members may not generate interest if the audience cannot relate to the accomplishments.

For many projects, results are not achieved until weeks or even months after the project are completed. Reinforcement is needed from many sources. Communicating results to a general audience may lead to motivation to continue the project or introduce similar ones in the future.

Stories about those involved in a project and the results they have achieved can help create a favorable image. Employees are made aware that the organization is investing resources to improve performance and prepare for the future. This type of story provides information about a project that may otherwise be unknown, and sometimes creates a desire for others to participate. Public recognition of project participants who deliver exceptional performance can enhance confidence and drive to excel.

Routine Feedback on Progress

A primary reason for collecting reaction and learning data is to provide feedback so that adjustments can be made throughout the project. For most interventions, data are routinely collected and quickly communicated to a variety of groups. A feedback action plan designed to provide information to several audiences using a variety of media may be an option. These feedback sessions may point out specific actions that need to be taken. This process becomes complex and must be managed in a very proactive manner. The following steps are recommended for providing feedback and managing the overall process. Many of the steps and concepts are based on the recommendations of Peter Block in his landmark book *Flawless Consulting*.

- **Communicate quickly.** Whether the news is good news or bad, it should be passed on to individuals involved in the project as soon as possible. The recommended time for providing feedback is usually a matter of days and certainly no longer than a week or two after the results become known.
- **Simplify the data.** Condense the data into an easily understandable, concise presentation. This is not the appropriate situation for detailed explanations and analysis.
- **Examine the role of the OD team and the client in the feedback process.** The OD team can wear many hats in the process. On the other hand, sometimes the client fills in roles that the OD team is used to carrying. These respective functions must be examined in terms of reactions to the data and the recommended actions.
- **Use negative data in a constructive way.** Some of the data will show that things are not going so well, and the fault may rest with the project leader or the client. In this case, the story basically changes from "Let's look at the success we've achieved," to "Now we know which areas to change."
- **Use positive data in a cautious way.** Positive data can be misleading, and if they are communicated too enthusiastically, they may create expectations that exceed what finally materializes. Positive data should be presented in a guarded way, allowing the response to be fully in the hands of the client.
- **Choose the language of the meeting and the communication carefully.** The language used should be descriptive, focused, specific, short, and simple. Language that is too judgmental, full of jargon, stereotypical, lengthy, or complex should be avoided.
- **Ask the client for reactions to the data.** After all, the client is the number one customer, and it is most important that the client be pleased with the project.
- **Ask the client for recommendations.** The client may have some good suggestions for what needs to be changed to keep a project on track, or to put it back on track should it derail.
- **Use support and confrontation carefully.** These two actions are not mutually exclusive. At times, support and confrontation are both needed for a particular group. The client may need support and yet be confronted for lack of improvement or sponsorship. The project team may be confronted regarding the problem areas that have developed, but may need support as well.
- **Act on the data.** The different alternatives and possibilities should be weighed carefully to arrive at necessary adjustments.

- **Secure agreement from all key stakeholders.** It is essential to ensure that everyone is willing to make suggested changes.
- **Keep the feedback process short.** We discourage allowing the process to become bogged down in long, drawn-out meetings or lengthy documents. If this occurs, stakeholders will avoid the process instead of being willing participants.

Following these steps will help move the project forward and generate useful feedback, often ensuring that adjustments are supported and can be executed.

THE COMMUNICATION PLAN

Any activity must be carefully planned to achieve maximum results. This is a critical part of communicating the results of the project. The actual planning of the communication is important to ensure that each audience receives the proper information at the right time and that necessary actions are taken. Several issues are crucial in planning the communication of results:

- What will be communicated?
- When will the data be communicated?
- How will the information be communicated?
- Where will the information be communicated?
- Who will communicate the information?
- Who is the target audience?
- What are the specific actions required or desired?

The communication plan is usually developed when the project is approved. This plan details how specific information is to be developed and communicated to various groups and the expected actions. In addition, this plan details how the overall results will be communicated, the time frame for communication, and the appropriate groups to receive the information. The OD project team leader, key managers, and stakeholders need to agree on the degree of detail in the plan.

An impact study can be used to present the results of a project. This is developed when a major project is completed and the overall, detailed results are known. Among the major questions to be answered in an impact study are who should receive the results and in what form. The impact study is more specialized than the plan for the overall project because it involves the final results of the project.

FINAL THOUGHTS

The final step in the ROI Methodology, communication of results, is a crucial step in the overall evaluation process. If this step is not executed adequately, the full impact of the results will not be recognized, and the study may amount to a waste of time. The chapter began with general dos and don'ts for communicating results; these can serve as a guide for any significant communication effort. The various target audiences were then discussed, with the most commonly used media for communicating project results. This chapter closed with a best practice report formula and components of a communication plan. In this next chapter, we will discuss how to sustain the momentum of evaluation and overcome barriers to using the methodology.

Implementing and Sustaining ROI

A change toward a higher level of group performance is frequently short-lived, after a "shot in the arm," group life soon returns to the previous level. This indicates that it does not suffice to define the objective of planned change in-group performance as the reaching of a different level. Permanency of the new level, or permanency for a desired period, should be included in the objective.

—*Kurt Lewin*

Kurt Lewin was born into a Jewish family in 1890 in Prussia. When Lewin was 15 years old, his family moved to Germany where he would stay till 1933. A man before his time, Lewin studied psychology, completing his doctoral degree in Berlin, and fought for women's rights while in Germany. But when Hitler came to power, Lewin fled to the United States. He quickly became a naturalized citizen and became associated with several affluent schools including Duke, Harvard, and Stanford University. Recognized by many today as the "founder of social psychology," he created the brilliant three-state change management model referred to as Unfreeze, Change, and Freeze. But it was Lewin's background of facing the challenge of adjusting to a completely different country, language, and culture that led him to become so intimate with change. He knew firsthand that change, in and of itself, was temporary if there was no plan or goal for the change to be sustained.

Even the best-designed process, model, or technique is worthless unless it is effectively and efficiently integrated into the organization. Often, change is not permanent for many reasons. One reason is resistance. As it relates to ROI, some of this resistance is based on fear and misunderstanding. Some is real, based on actual barriers and obstacles. Although the ROI process presented in this book is a step-by-step, methodical, and simplistic procedure, it can fail if it is not integrated properly, fully accepted, and supported by those who must make it work within the organization. This chapter focuses on some of the most effective means of overcoming resistance to implementing the ROI process in an organization.

THE IMPORTANCE OF SUSTAINING THE USE OF ROI

With any new process or change, there is resistance. Resistance may be especially great when implementing a process as complex as ROI. To implement ROI and sustain it as an important accountability tool, the resistance must be minimized or removed. Successful implementation essentially equates to overcoming resistance. Explained below are four key reasons to have a detailed plan in place to overcome resistance.

Resistance Is Always Present

Resistance to change is a constant. Sometimes, there are good reasons for resistance, but often it exists for the wrong reasons. The important point is to sort out both kinds of resistance and try to dispel the myths. When legitimate barriers are the basis for resistance, minimizing or removing them altogether is the challenge.

Implementation Is Key

As with any process, effective implementation is the key to its success. This occurs when the new technique, tool, or process is integrated into the routine framework. Without effective implementation, even the best process will fail. A process that is never removed from the shelf will never be understood, supported, or improved. Clear-cut steps must be in place for designing a comprehensive implementation process that will overcome resistance.

Implementation Requires Consistency

Consistency is an important consideration as the ROI process is implemented. With consistency come accuracy and reliability. The only way to make sure consistency is achieved is to follow clearly defined processes and procedures each time the ROI Methodology is used. Proper effective implementation will ensure that this occurs.

Implementation Requires Efficiency

Cost control and efficiency will be significant considerations in any major undertaking, and the ROI Methodology is no exception. During implementation, tasks must be completed efficiently and effectively. Doing so will help ensure that process costs are kept to a minimum, that time is used economically, and that the process remains affordable.

IMPLEMENTING THE PROCESS: OVERCOMING RESISTANCE

Resistance shows up in varied ways: in the form of comments, remarks, actions, or behaviors. Table 7-1 lists representative comments that indicate open resistance to the ROI process. Each comment signals an issue that must be resolved or addressed in some way. A few are based on realistic barriers, whereas others are based on myths that must be dispelled. Sometimes, resistance to the process reflects underlying concerns. For example, the project managers involved may fear losing control of their processes, and others may feel vulnerable to whatever action may follow if the project is not successful. Still others may be concerned about any process that brings change or requires the additional effort of learning.

Table 7-1. Typical Objections to Use of ROI Methodology

It costs too much.
It takes too much time.
Who is asking for this?
This is not in my job description.
I did not have input on this.
I do not understand this.
What happens when the results are negative?
How can we be consistent with this?
The ROI looks too subjective.
Our managers will not support this.
ROI is too narrowly focused.
This is not practical.

OD practitioners and team members may resist the ROI process and openly make comments similar to those listed in Table 7-1. It may take evidence of tangible and intangible benefits to convince team members that it is in their best interest to make the project a success. Although most clients do want to see the results of the project, they may have concerns about the information they are asked to provide and about whether their personal performance is being judged while the project is undergoing evaluation. Participants may express the very same fears listed in the table.

The challenge is to implement the methodology systematically and consistently so that it becomes normal business behavior and part of a routine and standard process built into projects. The implementation necessary to overcome resistance covers a variety of areas. Figure 7-1 shows actions outlined in this chapter that are presented as building blocks to overcoming resistance. They are all necessary to build the proper base or framework to dispel myths and remove or minimize barriers. The remainder of this chapter presents specific strategies and techniques devoted to each building block identified in Figure 7-1. They apply equally to the OD team and the client organization, and no attempt is made to separate the two in this presentation. In some situations, a particular strategy would work best with the OD team. In certain cases all strategies may be appropriate for both groups.

FIGURE 7-1. Building Blocks for Overcoming Resistance

Assessing the Climate

As a first step toward implementation, some organizations assess the current climate for achieving results. One way to do this is to develop a survey to determine current perspectives of the OD team and other stakeholders. Another way is to conduct interviews with key stakeholders to determine their willingness to follow the project through to ROI. With an awareness of the current status, the OD leads can plan for significant changes and pinpoint particular issues that need support as the ROI process is implemented.

DEVELOPING ROLES AND RESPONSIBILITIES

Defining and detailing specific roles and responsibilities for different groups and individuals addresses many of the resistance factors and helps pave a smooth path for implementation.

Identifying a Champion

As an early step in the process, one or more individual(s) should be designated as the internal leader or champion for the ROI Methodology. As in most change efforts, someone must take responsibility for ensuring that the process is implemented successfully. This leader serves as a champion for ROI and is usually the one who understands the process best and sees vast potential for its contribution. More important, this leader is willing to teach others and will work to sustain sponsorship.

Develop the ROI Leader

The ROI leader is usually a member of the OD team who has the responsibility for evaluation. For large organizations, the ROI leader may be part of HR or learning and development. This person holds a full-time position in larger project teams or a part-time position in smaller teams. Client organizations may also have an ROI leader who pursues the ROI Methodology from the client's perspective. The typical job title for a full-time ROI leader is manager or director of measurement and evaluation. Some organizations assign this responsibility to a team and empower it to lead the ROI effort.

In preparation for this assignment, individuals usually receive special training that builds specific skills and knowledge of the ROI process. The role of the implementation leader is quite broad and serves many specialized duties. In some organizations, the implementation leader can take on many roles, ranging from diagnostician to problem solver to communicator.

Leading the ROI process is a difficult and challenging assignment that requires unique skill. Fortunately, programs are available that teach these skills. For example, one such program is designed to certify individuals who will be assuming leadership roles in the implementation of the ROI Methodology. For more detail, see *www.roiinstitute.net*. This certification is built around 10 specific skill sets linked to successful ROI implementation, focusing on the critical areas of data collection, isolating the effects of the project, converting data to monetary value, presenting evaluation data, and building capability. This process is quite comprehensive but may be necessary to build the skills necessary for taking on this challenging assignment.

Establishing a Task Force

Making the ROI Methodology work well may require the use of a task force. A task force usually comprises a group of individuals from different parts of the project or client team who are willing to develop the ROI Methodology and implement it in the organization. The selection of the task force may involve volunteers, or participation may be mandatory depending on specific job responsibilities. The task force should represent the cross section necessary for accomplishing stated goals. Task forces have the additional advantage of bringing more people into the process and developing more ownership of and support for the ROI Methodology. The task force must be large enough to cover the key areas but not so large that it becomes too cumbersome to function. Six to 12 members is a good size.

Assigning Responsibilities

Determining specific responsibilities is critical because confusion can arise when individuals are unclear about their specific assignments in the ROI process.

Responsibilities apply to two areas. The first is the measurement and evaluation responsibility of the entire OD team. Everyone involved in OD projects may have some responsibility for measurement and evaluation. These responsibilities may include providing input on designing instruments, planning specific evaluations, analyzing data, and interpreting the results. Typical responsibilities include:

- ensuring that the initial analysis or diagnosis for the project includes specific business impact measures
- developing specific application and business impact objectives for the project
- keeping organization or team members focused on application and impact objectives
- communicating rationale and reasons for evaluation
- assisting in follow-up activities to capture application and business impact data
- providing assistance for data collection, data analysis, and reporting.

Although involving each member of the OD team in all these activities may not be appropriate, each individual should have at least one responsibility as part of his routine job duties. This assignment of responsibility keeps the ROI Methodology from being disjointed and separated during projects. More important, it brings accountability to those directly involved in implementation.

The assignment of responsibilities for evaluation requires attention throughout the evaluation process. Although the project team must be assigned specific responsibilities during an evaluation, requiring others to serve in support functions to help with data collection is not unusual. These responsibilities are defined when a particular evaluation strategy plan is developed and approved.

ESTABLISHING GOALS AND PLANS

Establishing goals, targets, and objectives is critical to the implementation, particularly when several OD projects are planned. The establishment of goals can include detailed planning documents for the overall process and for individual ROI projects. The next sections discuss aspects of the establishment of goals and plans.

Setting Evaluation Targets

Establishing specific targets for evaluation levels is an important way to make progress with measurement and evaluation. As emphasized throughout this book, not every OD intervention should be evaluated to ROI. Knowing in advance to which level the project will be evaluated helps in planning which measures will be needed and how detailed the evaluation must be at each level. Table 7-2 presents examples of targets set for evaluation at each level. The setting of targets should be completed early in the process with the full support of the entire project team. If practical and feasible, the targets should also have the approval of key managers—particularly the senior management team.

Table 7-2. Evaluation Targets in a Large Organization

Level	Target
Level 1, Reaction	100%
Level 2, Learning	80%
Level 3, Application and Implementation	40%
Level 4, Business Impact	25%
Level 5, ROI	10%

Developing a Plan for Implementation

An important part of implementation is establishing a timetable for the complete implementation of the ROI process. This document becomes a master plan for completion of the different elements presented earlier. Beginning with forming a team and concluding with meeting the targets previously described, this schedule is a project plan for transitioning from the present situation to the desired future situation. Items on the schedule include developing specific ROI projects, building staff skills, developing policy, and teaching managers the process. Figure 7-2 is an example of an implementation plan. The more detailed the document, the more useful it becomes. The project plan is a living, long-range document that should be reviewed frequently and adjusted as necessary. More important, those engaged in work on the ROI Methodology should always be familiar with the implementation plan.

Revising or Developing Guidelines and Procedures

Another part of planning is revising or developing the organization's policy or guidelines on OD measurement and evaluation. The guidelines document contains information developed specifically for the measurement and evaluation process. It is developed with input from the OD team and key managers or stakeholders. Sometimes, these guidelines are addressed during internal workshops designed to build measurement and evaluation skills. This statement addresses critical matters that will influence the effectiveness of the measurement and evaluation process. These may include adopting the five-level framework presented in this book, requiring Level 3 and 4 objectives for some or all interventions, and defining responsibilities for the OD team.

Figure 7-2. Implementation Plan for a Large Organization With Many Projects

	J	F	M	A	M	J	J	A	S	O	N	D	J	F	M	A	M	J	J	A	S	O	N
Team formed	■																						
Responsibilities defined	■																						
Policy developed		■	■	■																			
Targets set	■	■																					
Workshops developed			■	■	■	■	■																
ROI Project (A)				■	■	■	■	■	■														
ROI Project (B)						■	■	■	■	■	■	■	■										
ROI Project (C)									■	■	■	■	■	■	■								
ROI Project (D)											■	■	■	■	■	■	■	■	■	■			
Project teams trained								■	■	■	■	■	■										
Managers trained																	■	■	■	■			
Support tools developed				■	■																		
Guidelines developed		■	■	■	■	■																	

Guidelines are important because they provide structure and direction for the team and others who work closely with the ROI Methodology. These individuals keep the process clearly focused, and enable the group to establish goals for evaluation. Guidelines also provide an opportunity to communicate basic requirements and fundamentals of performance and accountability. More than anything else, they serve as learning tools to teach others, especially when they are developed in a collaborative way. If guidelines are developed in isolation, the team and management will be denied the sense of their ownership, making them neither effective nor useful.

Procedures for measurement and evaluation are important for showing how to use the tools and techniques, guide the design process, provide consistency in the ROI process, ensure that appropriate methods are used, and place the proper emphasis on each of the areas. The procedures are more technical than the guidelines and often include detailed steps showing how the process is undertaken and developed. They often include specific forms, instruments, and tools necessary to facilitate the process.

Preparing the OD Team

OD team members may resist the ROI Methodology. They often see evaluation as an unnecessary intrusion into their responsibilities that absorbs precious time and stifles creative freedom. The cartoon character Pogo perhaps characterized it best when he said, "We have met the enemy, and he is us." Several issues must be addressed when preparing the OD team for ROI implementation.

Involving the OD Team

For each key issue or major decision involving ROI implementation, the project team should be involved in the process. As evaluation guidelines are prepared and procedures are developed, team input is essential. Resistance is more difficult if the team helped design and develop the ROI process. Convene meetings, brainstorming sessions, and task forces to involve the team in every phase of developing the framework and supporting documents for ROI.

Using ROI as a Learning Tool

One reason the OD team may resist the ROI process is that the intervention's effectiveness will be fully exposed, putting the reputation of the team on the line. They may have a fear of failure. To overcome this, the ROI Methodology should be clearly positioned as a tool for learning, not a tool for evaluating project team performance (at least not during the early years of project implementation). Team members will not be interested in developing a process that may reflect unfavorably on their performance.

Evaluators can learn as much from failures as from success. If the intervention is not working, it is best to find out quickly so that issues can be understood firsthand, not from others. If the intervention is ineffective and not producing the desired results, the failure will eventually be known to clients and the management group (if they are not aware of it already). A lack of results will make managers less supportive of immediate and future projects. If the intervention's weaknesses are identified and adjustments quickly made, not only can more effective projects be developed, but also the credibility of and respect for project implementation can be enhanced.

Teaching the Team

The OD team and OD evaluator usually have inadequate skills in measurement and evaluation, and will need to develop some expertise. Measurement and evaluation are not always a formal part of the team's or evaluator's job preparation. Consequently, the OD team leader must learn ROI Methodology and its systematic steps; the evaluator must learn to develop an evaluation strategy and specific plan, to collect and analyze data from the evaluation, and to interpret results from data analysis.

INITIATING ROI STUDIES

The first tangible evidence of the value of using the ROI Methodology may be seen at the initiation of the first OD intervention for which an ROI calculation is planned. The next sections discuss aspects of identifying appropriate projects and keeping them on track.

Selecting the Initial Project

It is critical that appropriate interventions be selected for ROI analysis. Only certain types of projects qualify for comprehensive, detailed analysis. Characteristic of projects that are suitable for analysis are those that:

- involve large groups of participants
- are expected to have a long life cycle
- will be linked to major operational problems and opportunities upon completion
- are important to strategic objectives
- are expensive
- are time-consuming
- have high visibility
- have the interest of management in performing their evaluation.

Using these or similar criteria, the project leader must select the appropriate projects to consider for ROI evaluation. Ideally, sponsors should agree with or approve the criteria.

Developing the Planning Documents

Perhaps the two most useful ROI documents are the data collection plan and the ROI analysis plan. The data collection plan shows what data will be collected, the methods used, the sources, the timing, and the assignment of responsibilities. The ROI analysis plan shows how specific analyses will be conducted, including how to isolate the effects of the project and how to convert data to monetary values. Each evaluator should know how to develop these plans. Please refer to chapter 4 for more detail on these documents.

Reporting Progress

As the interventions are developed and the ROI implementation gets under way, status meetings should be conducted to report progress and discuss critical issues with appropriate team members. These meetings keep the OD team focused on the critical issues, generate the best ideas for addressing problems and barriers, and build a knowledge base for better implementation evaluation of future projects. Sometimes, these meetings are facilitated by an external consultant, perhaps an expert in the ROI process. In other cases, the project leader may facilitate. In essence, the meetings serve three major purposes: reporting progress, learning, and planning.

Establishing Discussion Groups

Because the ROI Methodology is considered difficult to understand and apply, establishing discussion groups to teach the process may be helpful. These groups can supplement formal workshops and other learning activities and are often very flexible in format. Groups are usually facilitated by an external ROI consultant or the project leader. In each session, a new topic is presented for a thorough discussion that should extend to how the topic applies to the organization. The process can be adjusted for different topics as new group needs arise, driving the issues. Ideally, participants in group discussions will have an opportunity to apply, explore, or research the topics between sessions. Group assignments, such as reviewing a case study or reading an article, are appropriate between sessions to further the development of knowledge and skills associated with the process.

Preparing the Clients and Executives

Perhaps no group is more important to the ROI process than the management team that must allocate resources for the intervention and support its implementation. In addition, the management team often provides input to and assistance for the ROI process. Preparing, training, and developing the management team should be carefully planned and executed.

One effective approach for preparing executives and managers for the ROI process is to conduct a briefing on ROI. Varying in duration from one hour to half a day, a practical briefing such as this can provide critical information and enhance support for ROI use. Managers leave these briefings with greater appreciation of the use of ROI and its potential impact on projects, and with a clearer understanding of their role in the ROI process. More important, they often renew their commitment to react to and use the data collected by the ROI Methodology.

A strong, dynamic relationship between the OD team and key managers is essential for successful implementation of the ROI Methodology. There must be a productive partnership that requires each party to understand the concerns, problems, and opportunities of the other. The development of such a beneficial relationship is a long-term process that must be deliberately planned for and initiated by key OD team members. The decision to commit resources and support to an intervention may be based on the effectiveness of this relationship.

Removing Obstacles

As the ROI Methodology is implemented, there will inevitably be obstacles to its progress. The obstacles are based on concerns discussed in this chapter, some of which may be valid, others of which may be based on unrealistic fears or misunderstandings.

Dispelling Myths

As part of the implementation, attempts should be made to dispel the myths and remove or minimize the barriers or obstacles. Much of the controversy regarding ROI stems from misunderstandings about what the process can and cannot do and how it can or should be implemented in an organization. After years of experience with ROI, and having noted reactions during hundreds of interventions and workshops, observers recognize many misunderstandings about ROI. These misunderstandings are listed below as myths about the ROI Methodology:

- ROI is too complex for most users.
- ROI is expensive and consumes too many critical resources.
- If senior management does not require ROI, there is no need to pursue it.
- ROI is a passing fad.
- ROI is only one type of data.
- ROI is not future-oriented; it only reflects past performance.
- ROI is rarely used by organizations.
- The ROI Methodology cannot be easily replicated.
- ROI is not a credible process; it is too subjective.
- ROI cannot be used with soft projects.
- Isolating the influence of other factors is not always possible.

- ROI is appropriate only for large organizations.
- No standards exist for the ROI Methodology.

Delivering Bad News

One of the obstacles perhaps most difficult to overcome is receiving inadequate, insufficient, or disappointing news. Addressing a bad-news situation is an issue for most project leaders and other stakeholders involved in a project The time to think about bad news is early in the process, but without ever losing sight of the value of the bad news. In essence, bad news means that things can change, that they need to change, and that the situation can improve. The team and others need to be convinced that good news can be found in a bad-news situation. Here is some advice to follow when delivering bad news:

- Never fail to recognize the power to learn and improve with a negative study.
- Look for red flags along the way.
- Lower outcome expectations with key stakeholders along the way.
- Look for data everywhere.
- Never alter the standards.
- Remain objective throughout the process.
- Prepare the team for the bad news.
- Consider different scenarios.
- Find out what went wrong.
- Adjust the story line to: "Now we have data that show how to make this program more successful." In an odd way, this puts a positive spin on data that are less than positive.

Using the Data

It is unfortunately too often the case that interventions are evaluated and significant data are collected, but nothing is done with the data. Failure to use data is a tremendous obstacle because once the intervention has concluded, the team has a tendency to move on to the next project or issue and get on with other priorities. Table 7-3 shows how the different levels of data can be used to improve projects. It is critical that the data be used—the data were essentially the justification for undertaking the project evaluation in the first place. Failure to use the data may mean that the entire evaluation was a waste. As the table illustrates, many reasons exist for collecting the data and using them after collection. These can become action items for the team to ensure that changes and adjustments are made. Also, the client or sponsor must act to ensure that the uses of data are appropriately addressed.

TABLE 7-3. Use of Evaluation Data

Use of Evaluation Data	Appropriate Level of Data				
	1	2	3	4	5
Adjust project design	✓	✓			
Improve implementation			✓	✓	
Influence application and impact			✓	✓	
Improve management support for the project			✓	✓	
Improve stakeholder satisfaction			✓	✓	✓
Recognize and reward participants		✓	✓	✓	
Justify or enhance budget				✓	✓
Reduce costs		✓	✓	✓	✓
Market projects in the future	✓		✓	✓	✓

Monitoring Progress

A final element of the implementation process is monitoring the overall progress made and communicating that progress. Although often overlooked, an effective communication plan can help keep the implementation on target and can let others know what the ROI Methodology is accomplishing for the OD team and the client. Elements of a communication plan were discussed in chapter 6.

The initial schedule for implementation of ROI is based on key events or milestones. Routine progress reports should be developed to communicate the status of these events or milestones. Reports are usually developed at six-month intervals but may be more frequent for short-term projects. Two target audiences, the project team and senior managers, are critical for progress reporting. All project team members should be kept informed of the progress, and senior managers should know the extent to which ROI is being implemented and how it is working within the organization.

FINAL THOUGHTS

Even the best model or process will die if it is not used and sustained. This chapter explored the implementation of the ROI process and ways to sustain its use. If not approached in a systematic, logical, and planned way, the ROI process will not be an integral part of the OD evaluation efforts, and accountability will consequently suffer. This chapter presented the different elements that must be considered and issues that must be addressed to ensure that implementation is smooth and uneventful. Smooth implementation is the most effective means of overcoming resistance to ROI. The result provides a complete integration of ROI as a mainstream component of major projects.

The first section of this book outlined the relevant steps necessary in using the ROI Methodology in OD interventions. In the next section of this book, we share three cases illustrating how the ROI process was applied to OD projects.

Part II

Evaluation in Action

Case Studies Describing the Evaluation of OD Interventions

8

Organization Culture Change

Agua Manufacturing Company

Lizette Zuniga, PhD

This case was prepared to serve as a basis for discussion rather than an illustration of either effective or ineffective administrative and management practices. All names, dates, places, and data may have been disguised at the request of the author or organization.

Abstract

This organizational culture change case study explores the details of the transition of a large manufacturing company (AMC) from a traditional organization to one that is marked by strong and empowering leadership, and an execution-friendly environment with clear strategy, goals, and priorities.

BACKGROUND

AMC is a large manufacturing company that serves an international customer base. Even in a slow economy, AMC has continued to increase revenues in the past several years, increasing its employee base by 25 percent. Although the company's revenue has grown, expenses incurred in the organization have been extraordinarily high and instead of enjoying a positive profit margin, the company has been in the red for the past three years. The leadership team met and discussed bringing in an external consultant to help understand underlying causes for these problems and look for course-correcting solutions.

ORGANIZATION ANALYSIS AND DIAGNOSTICS—ALIGNMENT AND DECISION TO CHANGE

The main purpose for conducting organization diagnostics was to understand the reasons for the problems the organization was having. It was during the initial consulting meeting that several methods were selected to collect data and more fully understand the concerns.

Capstone Organization Culture Assessment

The first method selected to understand the organization culture and potential area for change was the Capstone Organization Culture Assessment (Beard and Zuniga, 2006). This assessment was administered to gather data in the areas of leadership, decision making, values, planning, and structure. Approximately 700 were invited to participate and with 653 responding, the response rate was 93 percent. Some of the scores clustered near the mean, indicating a traditional organizational climate. AMC presents itself as an established organization, relying on the same products, services, and processes it has always used to remain successful. Given the changes in the marketplace and global economy, AMC cannot rely on business-as-usual practices. Currently, AMC does not appear to be a company poised for transformational growth. This kind of profile indicates status quo. The key findings were threefold:

1. **Leadership:** Scoring lowest in the leadership domain shows that this group of leaders is deficient in the areas of delegating and communicating with direct reports. The main leadership style is one with tendencies toward autocratic and tight management.
2. **Planning:** The planning domain scores also show gaps, specifically in unclear priorities, unclear goals, and no clear strategy.
3. **Decision Making:** The decision-making process is rather sluggish in getting decisions made, relying on a process to make decisions that involves getting buy-in from multiple parties and multiple layers.

Interviews With Key Individuals

While the assessment provided comprehensive information on major aspects of the company, it was not enough to draw conclusions about some of the primary concerns as well as underlying factors. To expedite the process, the assessment findings were used to generate a set of interview questions. This way, the questions were more targeted and specific to the company. Interviews were conducted with four executives, four members of the middle management team, and four non-supervisory team members to delve deeper and help specify gaps in performance and impact.

Five concerns were expressed:

- In the area of quality, they noted an increase in the number of errors made.
- In turnaround time to fulfill customer orders, orders were taking longer to complete; and therefore, more factories were reporting problems filling orders on time.

- With the increase in new employees, they needed more leaders prepared and poised for promotion.
- Given the change of the business and the fact that more change was needed, it was apparent that the existing leadership model was inadequate.
- They had experienced unusually high turnover.
- The most recent customer satisfaction survey indicated a marked decrease in customer satisfaction.

Figure 8-1 shows the Johari window created by Luft and Ingam (1955). In the Johari window, there are four aspects that describe an individual. When applied to organizations, the first domain is *open* for both insiders and outsiders to see. The second domain is *hidden* from outsiders but known to those on the inside. The third domain is one that the company doesn't see whereas an outsider could more readily see, otherwise known as *blind spots*. The fourth domain is one that neither the company nor an outsider readily sees, otherwise described as *unknown*. When using the concept of the Johari window in this case, the organizational features were plugged into the four quadrants to illustrate key aspects for this organization. Data from the initial meeting, organization culture assessment, and interview findings were used to populate what is seen in Figure 8-2.

Open

Several characteristics are apparent to insiders as well as outsiders. The company has been in business for several decades, and has an annual report that is made available internally as well as externally. The communication that exists is formal and written. This company has a reputation for being hardworking, possessing a strong work ethic, and as willing to do what it takes to fulfill the customer's request.

Hidden

Those who work for AMC are forthright about their reliance on their CEO and that there is no clear successor. They also are acutely aware that the CEO is nearing retirement age and there is heightened anxiety about this fact. Like the CEO, the executive team members also have no succession plan in place. In addition to there being no succession plan in place, there is no strategic plan that is communicated or known in the organization. Interviewees identified patterns of micro-management, tightly held supervision, and that employees felt a general sense of frustration.

FIGURE 8 -1. The Johari Window

	Known to self	Not known to self
Known to others	**Open**	**Blind Spots**
Unknown to others	**Hidden**	**Unknown**

FIGURE 8-2. The Johari Window Applied to Case

	Known to self	Not known to self
Known to others	**Open** • Public history • Formal communication • Strong work ethic • Customer driven	**Blind Spots** • Rigid thinking, keeping status quo • Cautious • Lack top-down communication
Unknown to others	**Hidden** • Productivity • Dependent on CEO • No strong successor • Lack clear direction • Micro-manage	**Unknown** • Lack of trust from leadership toward workforce • Workforce viewed as lazy, not pulling own weight

Blind Spots

The Capstone Organization Culture Assessment and the interviews revealed several areas that we categorized as blind spots. Culturally speaking, the unwritten rules that were operational in AMC formed expectations around acceptable risk, innovation, limited internal communication, and maintaining status quo. While AMC may not have been cognizant of these patterns, the collected data were confirming of these points.

Unknown

During the interviews, two underlying themes were noted. What was conveyed by the executive interviewees was confirmed by middle managers and non-supervisory team members. The two themes were:

- Leadership did not trust workforce.
- Leadership viewed workforce as lazy and not pulling their own weight.

These are categorized as *unknown* since they are not overtly expressed in the workplace. The unknown, in this case, is similar to Schein's description of underlying assumptions that are difficult to discern because they exist on an unconscious level (2010).

FEEDBACK GIVEN AND SOLUTION SELECTED

A report was generated that illustrated the findings from the interviews and the Capstone Organization Culture Assessment. While the report had conclusions and recommendations, a meeting was arranged between the consultant and the leadership team. It was during this meeting that findings were discussed and together, several key decisions were made. The decision was made to form a Guiding Coalition Group in the organization to assume responsibility for the changes that needed to be made. Realizing that resistance to change was likely, organizational readiness for change and flexibility were key, focusing on employees who were accountable to achieve results.

The Guiding Coalition was headed up by an executive champion and comprised of cross-functional employees with a mix of leaders and non-leaders. Under this group's direction, the organization took on the challenge of recreating itself by taking two significant steps:

1. **Master Action Planning Sessions:** The Guiding Coalition Group participated in strategic planning sessions, defining long-term and strategic plans and communicating those plans in the organization. Not only did the organization's scores on the assessment indicate that planning was a deficit, but they also could see consequences of operating their business in a "shoot-from-the-hip" modality. Three sub-groups emerged from this exercise, and each group was tasked with developing an action plan that would ultimately roll up to a Master Action Plan. The first group focused on initiatives to address the business needs

at hand, including reducing error, reducing time for order completion, and increasing customer satisfaction. The second group dedicated themselves to succession planning for the CEO and the executive team, reducing turnover, increasing the internal fill rate and promotability for leadership positions. The third group worked on devising a communication plan to support the change initiative. It was important to define and communicate the challenge, defining where the company was headed.

2. **Leadership Development:** This was going to be one of the toughest areas to tackle. Going from an autocratic style of management to one characterized as democratic or empowering was no easy feat. This fact led the OD team to create an innovative way to transform their leadership team. In addition to designing an eight-module leadership program, each leader was asked to create an action plan to implement new behaviors, which supported the Master Action Plan. Leaders were asked to work with their team of direct reports and identify solutions to one of four existing problems: 1) error rates, 2) turnaround time for order completion, 3) customer satisfaction, 4) turnover. The leaders were asked to lead these teams, not in an autocratic way, but in a democratic way—challenging the team to identify solutions to existing problems. Leaders were encouraged to use brainstorming, and in turn, they were to submit their team's findings to the Guiding Coalition Group. This helped foster an empowering type of leadership and atmosphere, while generating potential solutions for the Guiding Coalition Group.

DATA COLLECTION PLAN

Table 8-1 shows the data collection plan for the change management project. Multi-level objectives were created for Levels 1 through 5. The data collection plan shows targets for each level, along with timing of the data collection and who is responsible for collecting data at each level.

For Levels 1 and 2, two brief questionnaires were administered at the conclusion of the intervention and were used to collect reaction and learning data. The main items of concern for Level 1 are relevance and importance of the interventions, as well as action items identified through strategic planning and leadership development. For Level 2, the focus was on increasing knowledge and skills in leadership and planning.

Since the organization scored lower than average on leadership and planning, the main target for Level 3 was increasing organization planning behavior, changing the work effort to be aligned with the initiatives identified on the Master Action Plan, and improving leadership behaviors. Several sources of data were used to measure change in behavior. The main source of data, to examine whether the work effort was changing, was through the company's monthly progress reports. Additionally, action plans were used to gauge the degree that planning behaviors were being used in day-to-day jobs. The 360-degree feedback assessments were also used to measure leadership behaviors and progress made.

Internal HR and business databases were used to collect Level 4 data six months and one year after the intervention. Specifically, job satisfaction and turnover were collected from HR. Factories reporting problems with time to complete, error rates, and customer satisfaction were collected from the operations department through its business database.

ROI ANALYSIS PLAN

Table 8-2 shows the ROI Analysis Plan. For the Level 4 data items, two methods were used to isolate the effects of the intervention: 1) trend-line analysis and 2) estimates from the Guiding Coalition. In this case, historical data were projected in a trend and compared with the actual data to determine the impact. For error rates and turnover, estimates were also collected through a brief questionnaire from the Guiding Coalition to further corroborate the isolation factor.

Methods of converting data to money involved the use of standard values that had already been identified. The HR department already had identified standard values for turnover and the operations department had previously assigned standard values for error rates.

The project's fully loaded cost profile included the following: costs associated with diagnostics, which included conducting the Capstone Organization Culture Survey; the expense and time of those involved in conducting interviews; the two-fold intervention; facilities expense; administrative overhead; communication and evaluation costs.

Expected intangible benefits included improved communication, improved problem solving, and increased job satisfaction. Targets for communication and reporting were threefold, including the executive team, leadership team, and OD team.

Table 8-1. Data Collection Plan

Level	Objective(s)	Measures/Data	Data Collection Method	Data Sources	Timing	Responsibilities
1	**SATISFACTION/PLANNED ACTION** • Relevance to organization • Importance to organization success • Action items identified on Master Action Plan • Action items identified by leaders participating in leadership development	• Average of 4 on 5-point scale	• Questionnaire	• Guiding Coalition Group • Leaders participating in leadership development	• Immediately following: 1. strategic planning sessions 2. leadership development	• OD team
2	**LEARNING** • Enhancing leadership skills • Improving planning skills	• Average of 4 on 5-point scale	• Questionnaire	• Guiding Coalition Group • Leaders participating in leadership development	• Immediately following: 1. strategic planning sessions 2. leadership development	• OD team
3	**BEHAVIOR CHANGE** • Increase organization planning behavior • Improve leadership behaviors • Change work effort according to Master Action Plan	• Improvement made on Master Action Plan • Improved leadership behavior	• Master Action Plan update report • Action plan • 360° feedback report	• Guiding Coalition Group • Leaders participating in leadership development	• Six months after strategic planning and leadership development	• OD team

4	**BUSINESS IMPACT** • Increase customer satisfaction • Reduce number of factories reporting problems with time to fulfill customer orders • Reduce turnover • Reduce errors • Increase in promotions	• Reduce time to fulfill customer orders • Decrease turnover • Increase in promotion • Increase customer satisfaction • Reduce errors	• HR database • Quality database • Brief questionnaire	• Guiding Coalition Group • Leaders participating in leadership development	• Six months after strategic planning and leadership development	• OD team
5	**ROI** 25%	*Comments:* Action plans are provided and explained during leadership development program.				

TABLE 8-2. ROI Analysis Plan for Organization Culture Change Project

Intervention: Organization Culture Change Project **Responsibility:** Lizette Zuniga **Date:** ____________

Data Items (Usually Level 4)	Methods for Isolating the Effects of the Intervention	Methods of Converting Data to Monetary Values	Cost Categories	Intangible Benefits	Communication Targets for Final Report	Other Influences/ Issues During Application	Comments
• Reduction in errors	• Trend Line • Guiding Coalition's Estimates	• Standard value	• Diagnostics • Time of those involved in process • Strategic planning sessions • Leadership development initiative • 360° feedback • Administrative overhead • Communication expenses • Facilities • Evaluation	• Improved communication • Improved problem solving • Increased job satisfaction	• Executives • Guiding Coalition Group • Those involved in leadership development • OD team	• N/A	• There was overlap between those involved in strategic planning and those involved in leadership development
• Reduction in turnover	• Trend Line • Guiding Coalition's Estimates	• Standard value					
• Reduce reporting problems with filling customer orders on time	• Trend Line	• N/A					
• Increase customer satisfaction	• Trend Line	• N/A					
• Increase promotions	• Trend Line	• N/A					

RESULTS

Level 1, Reaction and Planned Action Results

A questionnaire was used to capture reaction data. Overall, the results were positive, indicating that the planning sessions and leadership development were timely and important for the future of the organization. Master Action Plans were created as a result of the planning intervention, and leadership action plans were created as a result of the leadership development initiative.

Level 2, Learning Results

In addition to the Level 1 items, the same questionnaire was used to collect Level 2 data. Items were included on the questionnaire that measured organization learning of leadership and knowledge and skills of planning.

Level 3, Behavior Change Results

The Master Action Plan reflected the specific organization initiatives and behaviors the group felt were necessary to affect the desired change. Six months after the plan was created, the OD team reviewed the monthly progress reports for months one through six to discern the change. Updates on the action plans created by leadership were also collected at the same time (after six months). Finally, 360-degree feedback data were also used to measure changes in awareness and leadership behaviors.

Level 4, Impact Results

The Level 4, Impact results were broken down into five categories, detailed below. See Table 8-3 for an overview of Level 4 results.

Factories Reporting Problems With Time-to-Order Completion

This measure was significant as it also affected customer satisfaction. In the beginning of the project, there was discussion as to the best way to report this measure. Every attempt was made to collect an average time for order completion, but after viewing the data and identifying the multiple types of orders and variations, it was decided that a meaningful way to track this item would be to show whether the trend went downward on the number of factories who reported problems with completing customer orders on time. The baseline showed that 31 factories reported problems with completing customer orders on time. Six months later, the number of factories went down to 18; one year later, the number of factories reporting problems with completing customer orders on time was six.

Error Rates

Error rates were tallied using common work practices of counting the number of error rates per 100. The average number of error rates was 35 per 100 at the start of this project. Six months later, it had decreased to 24 per 100. One year later, the number of error rates significantly decreased to seven per 100.

Turnover Costs

Although turnover had been traditionally low, in the last three years it had increased, due to significant changes in the workplace. One year after the intervention, turnover was reduced from 655 to 275. The trend-line analysis supported the turnover reduction.

Promotions

Trending data showed moderate improvement in promotions. The baseline was 5 percent prior to the intervention. One year later, the percent of promotions had increased to 18 percent.

Customer Satisfaction

Customer satisfaction surveys were conducted routinely in this organization. Two key items used for this project were:

- AMC moving aggressively to meet customer needs
- long-term commitment to AMC.

On both items, customer satisfaction increased. In the beginning of the project, 60 percent indicated that AMC moved to aggressively meet customer needs; whereas one year later, this number reached 82 percent. As for long-term commitment to AMC, 45 percent stated they were committed to a long-term relationship; whereas one year later, this figure was up to 68 percent.

Several intangible benefits were identified in the study and confirmed by actual input from responses on the questionnaire administered to the Guiding Coalition Group. The following benefits were realized as a result of the intervention:

- improved communication
- improved problem solving
- increased job satisfaction.

No attempt was made to place monetary values on any of the intangibles.

TABLE 8-3. Level 4 Measures

Level 4 Measure	Baseline (Before Intervention)	Six Months Later	One Year Later
Factories reporting problems with filling customer orders on time	31	18	6
Reduce error rates	35 errors per 100	24 errors per 100	7 errors per 100
Increase customer satisfaction	• 60% indicated they moved to aggressively meet customer needs • 45% said they were committed to long-term relationship	N/A	• 82% indicated they moved to aggressively meet customer needs • 68% said they were committed to long-term relationship
Reduce turnover	655	299	275
Increase promotions	5%	8%	18%

Level 5, ROI Results

The ROI results, Level 5, were calculated for costs and benefits.

Costs

Table 8-4 outlines the costs of the intervention. Calculating the cost of the intervention follows the categories outlined in the evaluation plan. For diagnostics, the total cost was $12,000. The strategic planning sessions were $112,000. Development and instructor time in leadership development were estimated at $550,000, and the 360-degree assessment costs were $25,000. The materials were $22,000, while a percentage for overhead was allocated to this intervention with an estimate of $1,500. Facilities, food, and refreshments came to $8,000; and since there were communication tasks and activities involved to help with change management, these costs were factored in, totaling $5,000.

The time involved for those in the Guiding Coalition and those participating in the leadership development program was also factored in. Salaries and benefits multiplied by the total time came to $95,000. The meeting room facilities, food, and refreshments were estimated at $8,000, while the evaluation costs were $18,500. Tallying all of these cost factors together brings the total to $849,000.

TABLE 8-4. Intervention Costs

Cost of Item	Cost
Diagnostics	$12,000
Strategic planning sessions	$112,000
Leadership development faculty/sessions	$550,000
360° assessment	$25,000
Program materials	$22,000
Overhead	$1,500
Facilities, food, and refreshments	$8,000
Communication	$5,000
Participant salaries (plus benefits) for time involved	$95,000
Evaluation costs	$18,500
TOTAL	**$849,000**

Benefits

The determination of monetary benefits for intervention was developed using the methods outlined in the ROI analysis plan. A standard value has routinely been used at AMC to reflect the cost of annual improvement value. As Table 8-5 illustrates, the error rates were converted based on a standard value of $750 per error. With 28 errors prevented each month, this yielded a $21,000 monthly improvement. When annualizing this improvement, the value is $252,000. After factoring in the average confidence percentage from the Guiding Coalition Group at 92 percent, the annual improvement is $231,840.

Value for Error Rates

$750 per error x 28 (change) = $21,000 (monthly)
$21,000 x 12 (months) = $252,000 (annual)
$252,000 x 92% (confidence %) = $231,840

The turnover rates were converted based on a standard value of $3,200 per unit of turnover. The majority of those who vacated their positions were in non-supervisory positions. Out-of-pocket expenses were the main cost categories that this organization used for costing turnover for non-supervisors. These categories included sign-on bonuses, recruitment, relocation, and severance. With 380 prevented during the year, this yielded an improvement value of $1,216,000. After factoring in the average confidence percentage from the Guiding Coalition Group, at 85 percent, the annual improvement is $1,033,600.

Value for Turnover

$3,200 per turnover x 380 (change) = $1,216,000

$1,216,000 x 85% (confidence %) = $1,033,600

TABLE 8-5. Monetized Benefits

	Annual Change in Measure	Unit Value	Annual Improvement Value	Guiding Coalition Group Confidence %	Adjustments Based on Confidence %
Error rates	336	$750	$252,000	92%	$231,840
Turnover	380	$3,200	$1,216,000	85%	$1,033,600

$$\text{ROI} = \frac{\$1,265,440-\$849,000}{\$849,000} = 49\%$$

CONCLUSIONS AND RECOMMENDATIONS

Several assumptions need to be mentioned in the discussion of conclusions and recommendations. One is that high turnover rates in a tight labor market can make the required hiring numbers an absolute barrier to growth plans. Another assumption made is that the main reason people leave their jobs is due to their relationship with their manager, and while this has been documented in research (Connaughton, 1999), it is not 100 percent certain that this is the primary reason for this organization. This assumption, nevertheless, is worth noting, due to the actions that were taken to develop the leadership pool. One final assumption to highlight is that the estimates collected by the Guiding Coalition Group were credible in isolating the effects of the solution. While a more objective method for isolating the effects was preferred (such as control group), the timing and rollout of the intervention did not allow for this approach in this case. When considering gathering estimates, out of all involved, this group appeared to be in the best position to assign estimates based on its depth of involvement in the project.

While this is a preliminary analysis of the impact of this culture change intervention, results from this study indicate that this intervention appears to be affecting turnover and error rates across the business in a significant way. Reports from the factories indicate a marked decrease among those reporting problems with filling customer orders in a timely manner. Customer satisfaction has also increased, noted on the two items that were particularly relevant for this study. From the action plans that were gathered from those participating in the leadership development initiative, improvement was made in communication and problem solving. Overall, the intervention is contributing to behavioral changes among those participating in the Guiding Coalition Group and the sub-group planning sessions.

For purposes of this study, the cost of turnover was a particularly conservative estimate. Cost factors for contract labor, sign on bonuses, referral bonuses, temp help, overtime, and training were not included in the turnover calculations.

Promotion data suggest that there has been a moderate increase. Ongoing collection of promotion data is highly recommended. Data that shows cross-business unit transfers is another way to assess the impact of this intervention.

Improved job satisfaction was identified as an intangible benefit that was desired. At the time of this report, the annual employee satisfaction survey was being prepared for company-wide distribution; therefore, there are no data available to report on this measure at this time.

Recommendations include continuing to track the impact of the intervention, including the job satisfaction data when it will be available. As organization culture change projects are long-term solutions and can take three to five years to take root in an organization and yield desirable change, there would be value in reviewing data collected after year two and year three of this intervention. To see if there is a marked difference in the organizational behaviors that were identified during the culture assessment and diagnostics phase, it is recommended to administer the assessment again after ample time has passed to assess whether these behaviors have changed. Preliminary and informal (anecdotal data) data confirm that the key organizational behaviors of leadership and planning had changed, and the ROI analysis confirms that major business metrics were favorably affected. These findings support that the intervention was a worthwhile effort.

QUESTIONS FOR DISCUSSION

1. For the remaining Level 4 improvement measures that were not converted to money, are there credible techniques to monetize these metrics? Which additional ones would you convert to money? Please explain.
2. Discuss alternatives for isolating the impact for this OD intervention.
3. Are there items of interest that warrant follow up or further understanding/ analysis? If yes, what are they, and what methods would you employ to follow up?
4. What is the best way to communicate these findings?
5. Would the methods used in this case study be relevant for a potential case in your organization? Why or why not?

ABOUT THE AUTHOR

Lizette Zuniga, PhD, brings more than 15 years of experience to the field of human resource development. She specializes in organization development, assessment, leadership development and measurement and evaluation. Dr. Zuniga co-authored the book *Costs and ROI: Evaluating at the Ultimate Level* with Jack Phillips and has published several articles and book chapters. She holds a master's degree in counseling psychology from Georgia State University, Atlanta, Georgia, and a PhD in leadership from Barry University, Miami, Florida.

9

Stress Management in Teams

Reducing Stress Management in Teams Midwest Electric, Inc.

Jack J. Phillips, PhD, and Patti P. Phillips, PhD

This case was prepared to serve as a basis for discussion rather than to illustrate either effective or ineffective administrative and management practices. All names, dates, places, and organizations have been disguised at the request of the author(s) or organization.

Abstract

Midwest Electric, Inc. (MEI) is a growing electric utility serving several Midwestern states. Since deregulation of the industry, MEI has been on a course of diversification and growth. Through a series of acquisitions, MEI has moved outside of its traditional operating areas and into several related businesses.

MEI has been experiencing significant workplace changes as it is transformed from a bureaucratic, sluggish organization into a lean, competitive force in the marketplace. These changes have placed tremendous pressure on employees to develop multiple skills and perform additional work. Employees, working in teams, must constantly strive to reduce costs, maintain excellent quality, boost productivity, and generate new and efficient ways to supply customers and improve service.

As with many industries in a deregulated environment, MEI has detected symptoms of employee stress. The safety and health function in the company suggested that employee stress has lowered productivity and reduced employee effectiveness. Stress is also considered to be a significant employee health risk. Research has shown that high levels of stress are commonplace in many work groups, and that organizations are taking steps to help employees and work groups reduce stress in many ways. The vice president of human resources has asked the training and education department, with the help of the safety and health department, to develop a program for work groups to help them alleviate stressful situations and deal more productively and effectively with job-induced stress.

Because of its size and sophisticated human resource systems, MEI has an extensive database on employee-related measures. MEI prides itself as being one of the leaders in the industry in human resources issues. Needs assessments are routinely conducted and the HR vice president is willing to allow sufficient time for an adequate needs assessment before proceeding with the program.

NEEDS ASSESSMENT

The overall purpose of the needs assessment was to identify the causes of a perceived problem. The needs assessment would:

- Confirm that a problem does exist and provide an assessment of the actual impact of this problem.
- Uncover potential causes of the problem within the work unit, company, and environment.
- Provide insight into potential remedies to correct the problem.

The sources of data for the needs assessment included company records, external research, team members, team leaders, and managers. The assessment began with a review of external research that identified the factors usually related to high stress and the consequences of high stress in work groups. The consequences uncovered specific measures that could be identified at MEI.

This external research led to a review of several key data items in company records including attitude surveys, medical claims, EAP utilization, safety and health records, and exit interviews. The attitude survey data represented the results from the previous year and were reviewed for low scores on the specific questions that could yield stress related symptoms. Medical claims were analyzed by codes to identify the extent of those related to stress induced illnesses. Employee Assistance Plan (EAP) data were reviewed to determine the extent to which employees were using provisions and services of the plan perceived to be stress related. Safety records were reviewed to determine if specific accidents were stress related or that causes of accidents could be traced to high levels of stress. In each of the above areas, the data were compared to the previous year to determine whether stress related measures were changing. Also, where available, data were compared to expected norms from the external research. Finally, exit interviews for the previous six months were analyzed to determine the extent to which the stress related situations were factors in an employee's decision to voluntarily leave MEI.

A small sample of employees (10 team members) was interviewed to discuss their work-life situations and uncover symptoms of stress at work. Also, a small group of managers (five) was interviewed with the same purpose. To provide more detail on this input, a 10 percent sample of employees received a questionnaire to explore the same issues. MEI has 22,550 employees with 18,220 non-supervisory team members.

SUMMARY OF FINDINGS

The needs assessment process uncovered several significant findings:

- There is evidence of high levels of stress in work groups caused by MEI's deregulation, restructuring, and job changes. In essence, the change in the nature of work has induced high levels of stress in most work groups.
- Stress has led to a deterioration in several performance measures including medical costs, short-term disability, withdrawals (absenteeism, turnover), and job satisfaction.
- Employees are often not fully aware of stress factors and the effect that it has on them and their work.
- Employees have inadequate skills for coping with stress and adjusting to, managing, and eliminating highly stressful situations.
- Managers have more insight into the causes of stress but do not have the skills or mechanisms to deal with most stressful situations.

PROGRAM PLANNING AND EVALUATION

Several inherent factors about work groups and data at MEI influenced the program and its subsequent evaluation. MEI is organized around teams where groups are not usually identical. However, many teams have similar performance measures. The HR database is rich with various measures and data on employees and work unit factors. Because of the team environment and the important role of the team leader/manager, the program to reduce stress must involve the management group in a proactive way. Any efforts to reduce stress must shift much of the responsibility to participants and thus reduce the amount of time off the job. Job pressures in the deregulated environment provide fewer off-the-job opportunities for meeting and development activities.

Program Design

While several approaches could be feasible to satisfy this need, four issues surfaced that influenced program design:

- A skills and knowledge deficiency exists and some type of learning event was necessary.

- Several stress management programs are commercially available which may avoid having to develop a new program from scratch.
- Managers need to be involved in the process to the greatest extent possible.
- Because of the concerns about time away from the job, the actual classroom/ formal meeting activities should be limited to one or two days.

With this in mind, the program outlined in Figure 9-1 was designed to meet this important need.

Why ROI?

HR/HRD training programs usually targeted for an ROI calculation are those perceived to be adding significant value to the company, and closely linked to the organizational goals and strategic objectives. The ROI calculation is then pursued to confirm the added value. Based on the results of the ROI analysis, these programs may be enhanced, redesigned, or eliminated if the ROI is negative. Stress management can be different. If the ROI analysis yields a negative value, the program may not be discontinued but may be altered for future sessions, particularly if behavior changes are not identified in the Level 3 evaluation.

At MEI, this program was chosen for a ROI calculation for two reasons. First, the HR and training and education departments were interested in the accountability of all programs, including stress management. Second, a positive ROI would clearly show management that these types of programs, which are preventive in nature, can significantly contribute to the bottom line when they are implemented and supported by management.

Because the program can be expensive if applied to the entire company, it was decided to try it on a limited basis to determine its success and then make a decision to adjust, discontinue, or expand the program to other areas in MEI. The ROI Methodology provides the best information to make that decision. Six groups were planned.

DATA COLLECTION PLAN

Figure 9-2 shows the data collection plan for the stress management program. Broad objectives were established for Levels 1, 2, 3, and 4 data collection. The data collection plan is comprehensive but necessary to meet all of the requirements at each of the four levels of data collection. The timing and responsibilities are detailed. For measuring learning, three tools were used. The StressMap® is one measure of learning in the awareness category. Completion of this provides insight into stress factors and stress signals. In addition, built into the one-day program is an end-of-course self-assessment

FIGURE 9-1. Stress Management for Intact Work Teams

Departments or work groups of 10 or more people who are committed to improving the satisfaction and effectiveness of their teams will benefit by this more comprehensive approach to stress. The process uses the StressMap tool as the starting point. Managers and representative employees will participate in focus groups to identify work satisfiers and stressors and then will collaborate on alleviating systemic sources of stress.

What Group Members Will Learn:

- Identify sources of stress and personal response to them.
- Individuals have the ability to make a difference in their lives.
- How to take the first steps to enhance personal health and overall performance.
- How to access resources, internally and externally, to help teach personal goals.

What the Group/Manager Will Learn:

- Group profile of sources of stress and response patterns.
- Additional information on sources of both work distress and work satisfaction will be obtained through focus groups. Themes will be identified where possible.
- New stress reduction skills specific to the needs of the group.
- Participate in development of recommendations for next steps to take to improve work satisfaction and productivity.

Highlights:

- Through completion of a comprehensive self-assessment tool called StressMap individuals will be able to immediately score themselves on 21 stress scales dealing with work and home life as well as learn about their preferred coping styles and the thinking and feeling patterns that affect their ability to manage stress. Anonymous copies of each member's StressMap will be compiled to create a group score.
- A 3-4 hour StressMap debriefing session designed to help individuals better interpret their scores will be followed by a four-hour module suited to the needs of the group (such as situation mastery, changing habits, creating climate for agreement). Total of one day.

Pre-course Requirements:

- Management commitment to the process. Employees to complete the StressMap tool and submit a confidential copy.

Length and Format:

- Lead time of three to four weeks minimum for preparation and communication.
- Consultant on site a day and a half.
- Initial follow-up one to two weeks later on site or by phone to senior management. Subsequent follow-up on impact of the initiative to occur as negotiated. Three to four hours of telephone follow-up included.

Cost:

- Approximately $xxxx (plus taxes) (USD) per group of eight to 25 and $xx (USD) per set of materials. Travel and living expenses for consultant are additional.

to measure learning. Finally, the facilitator has a brief checklist to indicate the extent of learning for the group.

At Level 3 data collection, the completion of the 21-day plan provides some evidence that the participants have changed behavior to reduce stress. A conference call is planned with the facilitator, team manager, and the team 21 days after the course. The call provides a review of issues and addresses any concerns or barriers to further implementation. A follow-up session is planned with the team, co-facilitated by the manager and facilitator, approximately one to two weeks after the one-day program, to discuss changes in behavior and address barriers. To determine the extent to which the participants are using internal or external resources to address stress related problems, records of those requests will be reviewed for approximately six months. Finally, a detailed follow-up questionnaire is planned six months after the program to collect both Level 3 and 4 data. This questionnaire will capture sustained behavior changes, indicate barriers to improvement, and identify impact measures for both groups and individuals.

Group records reveal changes in medical costs, absenteeism, turnover, and productivity six months after the program. In addition, increased job satisfaction will be determined from the follow-up questionnaire which will be administered six months after the program (i.e., the same questionnaire described earlier).

ROI ANALYSIS PLAN

Figure 9-3 shows the ROI Analysis Plan. For most data items, the method to isolate the effects of training will be obtained in a control group arrangement where the performance of the group involved in the program will be compared to a carefully matched companion control group. In addition, for most of the data items, trend-line analysis will be utilized. Historical data are projected in a trend and compared with the actual data to determine the impact of the program.

The methods of converting data involve a variety of approaches including tabulation of direct costs, using standard values, using external data, and securing estimates from different target audiences. The cost categories represent fully loaded costs for the program. Expected intangible benefits from the program are based on the experience of other organizations and other stress reduction programs. The communication target audience shows six key groups ranging from corporate and business unit managers to participants and their immediate supervisors.

FIGURE 9-2. Evaluation Plan: Data Collection

Program: Stress Management for Intact Groups **Responsibility:** Jack Phillips **Date:** January 15, 1997

Level	Broad Program Objective(s)	Data Collection Method	Timing of Data Collection	Responsibilities for Data Collection
I Reaction, Satisfaction, and Planned Actions	• Positive reaction • Suggestions for improvements • Planned action	• Standard questionnaire • 21-day action plan	• End of one-day course • End of course	• Facilitator • Facilitator
II Learning	• Personal stress awareness • Coping strategies • Stress reduction skills	• StressMap • Self-assessment • Facilitator assessment	• Prior to course • End of course • End of course	• Facilitator • Facilitator • Facilitator
III Job Application	• Change behavior to reduce stress • Develop group action plan and communicate to group • Access internal/external resources • Application of skills/knowledge	• Completion of 21-day plan • Conference call • Follow-up session • Review records • Follow-up questionnaire	• 21 days after course • 21 days after course • 1-2 weeks after one-day course • 6 months after course • 6 months after course	• No report • Facilitator • Facilitator/Manager • Program coordinator • External consultant
IV Business Impact	• Reduce medical care costs • Reduce absenteeism • Reduce turnover • Increase productivity • Increase job satisfaction	• Group records • Group records • Group records • Group records • Follow-up questionnaire	• 6 months after course • 6 months after course • 6 months after course • 6 months after course • 6 months after course	• Program coordinator • Program coordinator • Program coordinator • Program coordinator • External consultant

FIGURE 9-3. Evaluation Plan: ROI Analysis

Program: Stress Management for Intact Groups **Responsibility:** Jack Phillips **Date:** January 15, 1997

Data Items	Methods of Isolating the Effects of the Program	Methods of Converting Data	Cost Categories	Intangible Benefits	Other Influences/ Issues	Communication Targets
Medical healthcare costs; preventable claims	• Control group arrangement • Trend-line analysis	• Direct costs	• Needs assessment • Program development • Program materials • Participant salaries/benefits • Participant travel (if applicable) • Facilitator • Meeting facilities (room, food, beverages) • Program coordinator • Training and education overhead • Evaluation costs	• Improved communication • Time savings • Fewer conflicts • Teamwork • Improvement in problem solving	• Match groups appropriately • Limit communication with control group • Check for team building initiatives during program • Monitor restructuring activities during program • 6 groups will be monitored	• Program participants • Intact team/ manager • Senior manager/ management in business units • Training and education staff • Safety and health staff • Senior corporate management • Prospective team leaders
Absenteeism	• Control group arrangement • Trend-line analysis	• Supervisor estimation • Standard value				
Employee turnover	• Control group arrangement • Trend-line analysis	• External study—cost of turnover in high-tech industry • Management review				
Employee job satisfaction	• Control group arrangement • Management estimation	• Management estimation				
Employee/ Group productivity	• Control group arrangement • Trend-line analysis	• Standard values • Management estimation				

FIGURE 9-4. Manager Input: Potential Area for Improvement

Stress Reduction for Intact Work Teams

Before you begin the Stress Reduction program for your team, it is important to capture specific concerns that you have about your work group. Some of these concerns may be stress related and consequently may be used to help structure specific goals and objectives for your team. For each of the following potential areas of improvement, please check all that apply to your group. Add others if appropriate. Next to the item provide specific comments to detail your concerns and indicate if you think that this concern may be related to excessive stress.

❑	**Employee Turnover.** *Comments:*
❑	**Employee Absenteeism.** *Comments:*
❑	**Employee Complaints.** *Comments:*
❑	**Morale/Job Satisfaction.** *Comments:*
❑	**Conflicts With the Team.** *Comments:*
❑	**Productivity.** *Comments:*
❑	**Quality.** *Comments:*
❑	**Customer Satisfaction.** *Comments:*
❑	**Customer Service.** *Comments:*
❑	**Work Backlog.** *Comments:*
❑	**Delays.** *Comments:*
❑	**Other Areas.** *List and Provide Comments:*

FIGURE 9-5. Manager Responsibility and Involvement

Stress Management for Intact Work Teams With the team approach, the team manager should:	
1.	Have a discussion with the trainer to share reasons for interest in stress reduction and the desired outcome of the program. Gain a greater understanding of the StressMap and the OD approach. Discuss recent changes in the work group and identify any known stressors. This meeting could be held with the senior manager or the senior management team.
2.	Identify any additional work group members for the consultant to call to gather preliminary information.
3.	Appoint a project coordinator, preferably an individual with good organizing and influencing skills who is respected by the work group.
4.	Send out a letter inviting the group to participate in the program with personal endorsement and signature.
5.	Allocate eight hours of work time per employee for completion of StressMap and attendance at a StressMap debriefing and customized course.
6.	Schedule a focus group after discussing desired group composition with the facilitator. Ideal size is 10 to 22 participants. Manager should not attend.
7.	Attend the workshop and ensure that direct reports attend.
8.	Participate in the follow-up meeting held after the last workshop, either in person or by conference call. Other participants to include are the HR representative for your area, the safety and health representative for your area, and your management team. The trainer will provide you feedback about the groups' issues and make recommendations of actions to take to reduce work stress or increase work satisfaction.
9.	Commit to an action plan to reduce workplace distress and increase workplace satisfaction after thoughtfully considering feedback.
10.	Communicate the action plan to your work group.
11.	Schedule and participate in a 21-day follow-up call with the consultant and your work group.
12.	Work with your team (managers, HR, safety and health, facilitator) to evaluate the success of the action plan and determine next steps.

MANAGEMENT INVOLVEMENT

Management involvement was a key issue from the very beginning and was integrated throughout the design of the program. The manager serves as the team leader for the program, although a facilitator provides assistance and conducts a one-day workshop. Figure 9-4 illustrates the tool used for identifying initial problems as the work group began utilizing the Stress Management program. With this brief questionnaire, the manager identifies specific problem areas and provides appropriate comments and details. This exercise allows program planning to focus on the problems and provides guidance to the facilitator and the team.

Manager responsibility and involvement for the process is illustrated in Figure 9-5. This handout, provided directly to the managers, details 12 specific areas of responsibility and involvement for the managers. Collectively, initial planning, program design, and detailing of responsibilities pushed the manager into a higher profile position in the program.

CONTROL GROUP ARRANGEMENT

The appropriateness of control groups was reviewed in this setting. If a stress reduction program is needed, it would be appropriate and ethical to withhold the program for certain groups while the experiment is being conducted. It was concluded that this approach was appropriate because the impact of the planned program was in question. Although it was clear that stress-induced problems exist at MEI, there was no guarantee that this program would correct them. Six control groups were planned. The control group arrangement was diligently pursued because it represented the best approach to isolate the effects of the program, if the groups could be matched.

Several criteria were available for group selection. Figure 9-6 shows the data collection instrument used to identify groups for a control group arrangement. At the first cut, only those groups that had the same measures were considered (for example, at least 75 percent of the measures were common in the group). This action provided an opportunity to compare performance in the six months preceding the program.

Next, only groups in the same function code were used. At MEI, all groups were assigned a code depending on the type of work, such as finance and accounting or engineering. Thus, each experimental group had to be in the same code as the matched control group. It was also required that all six groups be spread over at least three different codes.

Two other variables were used in the matching process: group size and tenure. The number of employees in the groups had to be within a 20 percent spread and the average tenure had to be within a two-year range. At MEI, as with many other utilities, there is a very high average tenure rate.

Although other variables could be used to make the match, these five were considered to be the most influential in the outcome. In summary, the following criteria were used to select the two sets of groups:

- same measures of performance
- similar performance in the previous six months
- same function code

- similar size
- similar tenure.

The six pairs of groups represented a total level of employment of 138 team members for the experimental groups, and 132 team members and six managers for the control groups.

DATA COLLECTION

Figure 9-7 shows the data collection instrument for participants. A similar, slightly modified instrument was used with the managers. In all, 73 percent of the participants returned the questionnaire. This excellent response rate is due, in part, to a variety of actions taken to ensure an appropriate response rate. Some of the most important actions were:

- The team manager distributed the questionnaire and encouraged participants to return it to the external consulting firm. The manager also provided a follow-up reminder.
- A full explanation of how the evaluation data would be utilized was provided to participants.
- The questionnaire was reviewed during the follow-up session.
- Two types of incentives were used.
- Participants were promised a copy of the questionnaire results.

RESULTS: APPLICATION

The application of the program was considered an outstanding success with 92 percent of the participants completing their 21-day action plan. A conference call at the end of the 21 days showed positive feedback and much enthusiasm for the progress made. The follow-up session also demonstrated success, because most of the participants had indicated changes in behavior.

The most comprehensive application data came from the six-month questionnaire administered to participants and managers. The following skills and behaviors were reported as achieving significant success:

- taking full responsibility for your actions
- identifying or removing barriers to change behavior
- applying coping strategies to manage stressful situations
- responding effectively to conflict
- creating a positive climate
- acknowledging a complaint properly.

Figure 9-6. Manager Input: Group Measures and Characteristics

To measure the progress of your team, a brief profile of performance measures for employees and your work group is needed. This information will be helpful to determine the feasibility of using your group in a pilot study to measure the impact of the Stress Management program. Changes in performance measures will be monitored for six months after the program.

Listed below are several categories of measures for your work group. Check the appropriate category and please indicate the specific measure under the description. In addition, indicate if it is a group measure or an individual measure. If other measures are available in other categories, please include them under "Other."

Key Performance Measures Dept.________________

Performance Category	Measure	Description of Measure	Group Measure	Individual Measure
Productivity	1.		❑	❑
	2.		❑	❑
Efficiency	3.		❑	❑
	4.		❑	❑
Quality	5.		❑	❑
	6.		❑	❑
Response Time	7.		❑	❑
	8.		❑	❑
Cost Control/ Budgets	9.		❑	❑
	10.		❑	❑
Customer Satisfaction	11.		❑	❑
	12.		❑	❑
Absenteeism Turnover	13.		❑	❑
	14.		❑	❑
Morale/ Job Satisfaction	15.		❑	❑
	16.		❑	❑
Other (Please specify)	17.		❑	❑
	18.		❑	❑
	19.		❑	❑
	20.		❑	❑

Group Characteristics

Average tenure for group ______ years.

Average job grade for group ________.

Number in group _________.

Co-workers were the most frequently cited group in which relationships had improved through use of the skills, with 95 percent indicating application improvement with this group.

Barriers

Information collected throughout the process, including the two follow-up questionnaires, indicated few barriers to implementing the process. The two most frequently listed barriers were:

- There was not enough time.
- The work environment does not support the process.

Management Support

Manager support seemed to be quite effective. The most frequently listed behaviors of managers were:

- Managers set goals for change and improvement.
- Managers discussed how the program can apply to the work group.

RESULTS: IMPACT

The impact of the program was very significant with regard to both perceptions and actual values. On Figure 9-7, the follow-up questionnaire, 90 percent of the participants perceived this program as a good investment for MEI. In addition, participants perceived that this program had a significant influence on:

- employee satisfaction
- absenteeism
- turnover
- healthcare cost
- safety and health cost.

This assessment appears to support the actual improvement data outlined below. For each measure below, only the team data were collected and presented. Since managers were not the target of the program, manager performance data were not included. An average of months five and six was used consistently for the post-program data analysis, instead of the sixth month, to eliminate the spike effect.

Healthcare Costs

Healthcare costs for employees were categorized by diagnostic code; thus, it was a simple process to track the cost of stress-induced illnesses. Although there were few differences shown in the first three months after the program began, by month five and six an average difference of $120 per employee per month was identified. This was apparently due to the lack of stress-related incidents and the subsequent medical costs resulting from the stress. It was believed that this amount would be an appropriate improvement to use. The trend-line projection of healthcare costs was inconclusive because of the variability of the medical care costs prior to the program. A consistent trend could not be identified.

Absenteeism

There were significant differences of absenteeism in the two groups. The average absenteeism for the control group for months five and six was 4.65 percent. The absenteeism rate for the groups involved in the program was 3.2 percent. Employees worked an average of 220 days. The trend-line analysis appeared to support the absenteeism reduction. Because no other issues were identified that could have influenced absenteeism during this time period, the trend-line analysis provided an accurate estimate of the impact.

Turnover Costs

Although turnover at MEI was traditionally low, in the last two years it had increased due to significant changes in the workplace. A turnover reduction was identified using the differences in the control group and experimental group. The control group had an average annual turnover rate for months five and six of 19.2 percent. The experimental group had an average of 14.1 percent for the same two months. As with absenteeism, the trend-line analysis supported the turnover reduction.

Productivity

Control group differences showed no significant improvement in productivity. Of all the measures collected, the productivity measure was the most difficult to match between the two groups, which may account for the inconclusive results. Also, the trend line differences showed some slight improvement, but not enough to develop an actual value for productivity changes.

Job Satisfaction

Because of the timing difference in collecting attitude survey data, complete job satisfaction data were not available. Participants did provide input on the extent to which they felt the program actually influenced job satisfaction. The results were very positive, with a significant influence rating for that variable. Because of the subjective nature of job satisfaction and the difficulties with measurement, a value was not assigned to job satisfaction.

FIGURE 9-7. Stress Management for Intact Work Teams Impact Questionaire

Check one: ❑ Team Member ❑ Team Leader/Manager

1. Listed below are the objectives of the Stress Management program. After reflecting on this program, please indicate the degree of success in meeting the objectives.

OBJECTIVES	Failed	Limited Success	Generally Successful	Completely Successful
PERSONAL • Identify sources of stress in work, personal, and family worlds.				
• Apply coping strategies to manage stressful situations.				
• Understand to what degree stress is hampering your health and performance.				
• Take steps to enhance personal health and overall performance.				
• Access internal and external resources to help reach personal goals.				
GROUP • Identify sources of stress for group.				
• Identify sources of distress and satisfaction.				
• Apply skills to manage and reduce stress in work group.				
• Develop action plan to improve work group effectiveness.				
• Improve effectiveness and efficiency measures for work group.				

2. Did you develop and implement a 21-day action plan? Yes ❑ No ❑

If yes, please describe the success of the plan. If not, explain why.

---

3. Please rate, on a scale of 1-5, the relevance of each of the program elements to your job, with (1) indicating no relevance, and (5) indicating very relevant.

StressMap® Instrument___ Action Planning___ Group Discussion___ Program Content___

4. Please indicate the degree of success in applying the following skills and behaviors as a result of your participation in the Stress Management program.

	1	2	3	4	5	6
	No	**Little**	**Some**	**Significant**	**Very Much**	**No Opportunity to Use Skills**
a) Selecting containable behavior for change						
b) Identify measures of behavior						
c) Taking full responsibility for your actions						
d) Selecting a buddy to help you change behavior						
e) Identifying and removing barriers to changing behavior						
f) Identifying and using enablers to help change behavior						
g) Staying on track with the 21-day action plan						
h) Applying coping strategies to manage stressful situations						
i) Using control effectively						
j) Knowing when to let go						
k) Responding effectively to conflict						
l) Creating a positive climate						
m) Acknowledging a complaint properly						
n) Reframing problems						
o) Using stress talk strategies						

5. List (3) behaviors or skills you have used most as a result of the Stress Management program.

____

____

____

6. When did you first use one of the skills from the program?

- ❑ During the program
- ❑ Day(s) after the program (indicate number)
- ❑ Week(s) after the program (indicate number)

7. Indicate the types of relationships where you have used the skills.

- ❑ Co-workers
- ❑ Manager or supervisor
- ❑ MEI employee in another function
- ❑ Spouse
- ❑ Child
- ❑ Friend
- ❑ Other: (list) ______________________

PERSONAL CHANGES

8. What has changed about your on-the-job behavior as a result of this program? (positive attitude, fewer conflicts, better organized, fewer outbursts of anger, etc.)

____

____

____

9. Recognizing the changes in your own behavior and perceptions, please identify any specific personal accomplishments/improvements that you can link to this program (time savings, project completion, fewer mistakes, etc.)

____

____

____

10. What specific value in U.S. dollars can be attributed to the above accomplishments/ improvements? While this is a difficult question, try to think of specific ways in which the above improvements can be converted to monetary units. Use one year of data. Along with the monetary value, please indicate the basis of your calculation.

$__________

Basis ____

____

11. What level of confidence do you place on the above estimations? (0% = No Confidence, 100% = Certainty) __________%

12. Other factors often influence improvements in performance. Please indicate the percent of the above improvement that is related directly to this program. ____________%

Please explain.

____
____
____

GROUP CHANGES

13. What has changed about your work group as a result of your group's participation in this program? (interactions, cooperation, commitment, problem solving, creativity, etc.)

14. Please identify any specific group accomplishments/improvements that you can link to the program (project completion, response times, innovative approaches).

15. What specific value in U.S. dollars can be attributed to the above accomplishments/improvements? While this is a difficult question, try to think of specific ways in which the above improvements can be converted to monetary units. Use one year of values. Along with the monetary value, please indicate the basis of your calculation.
$____________

Basis ____
____

16. What level of confidence do you place on the above estimations? (0% = No Confidence, 100% = Certainty) ____________%

17. Other factors often influence improvements in performance. Please indicate the percent of the above improvement that is related directly to this program. ____________%

Please explain.

____
____
____

18. Do you think this program represented a good investment for MEI?
Yes ❑ No ❑

Please explain.

____
____

19. What barriers, if any, have you encountered that have prevented you from using skills or knowledge gained in this program? Check all that apply. Please explain, if possible.

- ❑ Not enough time
- ❑ The work environment doesn't support it
- ❑ Management doesn't support it
- ❑ The information is not useful (comments)
- ❑ Other ___________________________________

20. Which of the following best describes the actions of your manager during the Stress Management program.

- ❑ Very little discussion or reference to the program.
- ❑ Casual mention of program with few specifics.
- ❑ Discussed details of program in terms of content, issues, concerns, etc.
- ❑ Discussed how the program could be applied to work group.
- ❑ Set goals for changes/improvements.
- ❑ Provided ongoing feedback on the action plan.
- ❑ Provided encouragement and support to help change behavior.
- ❑ Other (comments) ___________________________________

____

21. For each of the areas below, indicate the extent to which you think this program has influenced these measures in your work group.

	1	2	3	4	5
	No Influence	**Some Influence**	**Moderate Influence**	**Significant Influence**	**Very Much Influence**
a) Productivity					
b) Efficiency					
c) Quality					
d) Response Time					
e) Cost Control					
f) Customer Service					
g) Customer Satisfaction					
h) Employee Turnover					
i) Absenteeism					
j) Employee Satisfaction					
k) Healthcare Costs					
l) Safety and Health Costs					

22. What specific suggestions do you have for improving the Stress Management program? Please specify.
    - ❑ Content____________________
    - ❑ Duration____________________
    - ❑ Presentation____________________
    - ❑ Other____________________

23. Other comments:

____
____
____

RESULTS: INTANGIBLE BENEFITS

Several intangible benefits were identified in the study and confirmed by actual input from participants and questionnaires. The following benefits were pinpointed:

- employee satisfaction
- teamwork
- improved relationships with family and friends
- time savings
- improved image in the company
- fewer conflicts.

No attempt was made to place monetary values on any of the intangibles.

MONETARY VALUES

The determination of monetary benefits for the program were developed using the methods outlined in the ROI analysis plan. A standard value has routinely been used at MEI to reflect the cost of an absence. The value is 1.25 times the average daily wage rate. For the experimental group, the average wage rate was $123 per day. The six team managers estimated a larger value of $174. For employee turnover, several turnover cost studies are available which reveal a value of 85 percent of annual base pay. As expected, senior managers felt that this cost of turnover was slightly overstated and preferred to use a value of 70 percent. The total economic benefits are illustrated in Table 9-1.

TABLE 9-1. Annual Monetary Benefits for 138 Participants

	Monthly Difference	Unit Value	Annual Improvement Value
Medical Costs	$120	- - -	$198,720
Absenteeism	1.45%	$153.75	$67,684
Turnover	5.1% (annualized)	$22,386	$157,553
		TOTAL	**$423,957**

The medical costs are converted directly. A $120 per month savings yields a $198,720 annual benefit. Other values are as follows:

Unit Value for an Absence

$123 x 1.25 = $153.75

Unit Value for Turnover

$31,980 x 70% = $22,386

Improvement for Absenteeism

138 employees x 220 workdays x 1.45% x $153.75 = $67,684

Improvement for Turnover

138 employees x 5.1% x $22,386 = $157,553

No values were used for productivity or job satisfaction.

PROGRAM COSTS

Calculating the cost of the program follows the categories outlined in the evaluation plan. For needs assessment, all of the costs were fully allocated to the six groups. Although the needs assessment was necessary, the total cost of needs assessment, $16,500, was included. All program development costs were estimated at $4,800. The program could possibly be spread through other parts of the organization which would ultimately be prorated across all the sessions. However, the costs were low because the materials were readily available for most of the effort and the total development cost was used. The program materials were $95 per participant.

The salaries for the team members averaged $31,980, while the six team managers had average salaries of $49,140. The benefits factor for MEI is 37 percent for both groups. Although the program took a little more than one day of staff time, one day of program time was considered sufficient for cost. The participant's travel cost ($38 per participant) was very low because the programs were conducted in the area. The facilitator cost, program coordination, and training and development overhead costs were estimated to be $10,800. The meeting room facilities, food, and refreshments averaged $22 per participant. Evaluation costs were $22,320. It was decided that all of the evaluation costs would be allocated to these six groups. This determination was extremely conservative since the evaluation costs could be prorated if the program was implemented over other areas. The costs for the program are detailed in Table 9-2. The costs were considered to be fully loaded with no proration except for needs assessment. Additional time could have been used for participants' off-the-job activities. However, it was concluded one day should be sufficient (for the one-day program).

TABLE 9-2. Program Costs

Cost Category	Total Cost
Needs Assessment	16,500
Program Development	4,800
Program Materials (144 x $95)	13,680
Participant Salaries / Benefits Based on 1 day (138 x $123 x 1.37 and 6 x 189 x 1.37)	24,108
Travel and Lodging (144 x 38)	5,472
Facilitation, Coordination, T&E Overhead	10,800
Meeting Room, Food, and Refreshments (144 x 22)	3,168
Evaluation Costs	22,320
TOTAL	**$100,848**

RESULTS: ROI

The return on investment and the benefit-cost ratio are shown below.

$$BCR = \frac{\$423{,}957}{\$100{,}848} = 4.20$$

$$ROI = \frac{\$423{,}957 - \$100{,}848}{\$100{,}848} = 320\%$$

Although this number is considered to be very large, it is still conservative because of the following assumptions and adjustments:

- Only first year values have been used. The program should actually have second and third year benefits.
- Control group differences were used in the analysis which is often the most effective way to isolate the effects of the program. These differences were also confirmed with the trend-line analysis.
- The participants provided additional monetary benefits, detailed on the questionnaires. Although they could have been added to the total numbers, these benefits were not included since only 23 participants of the 144 supplied values for those questions.
- The costs are fully loaded.

When considering these adjustments, the value should represent a realistic value calculation for the actual return on investment.

COMMUNICATION STRATEGIES

The communication follows the strategy outlined in Table 9-3. Three separate documents were developed to communicate with the different target groups in a variety of ways.

POLICY AND PRACTICE IMPLICATIONS

Because of the significance of the study and the information, two issues became policy. Whenever programs are considered that involve large groups of employees or a significant investment of funds, a detailed needs assessment will be conducted to ensure that the proper program is developed. Also, an ROI study is conducted for a small group of programs to measure the impact before complete implementation. In essence, this influenced the policy and practice on needs assessment, pilot program evaluation, and the number of impact studies developed.

TABLE 9-3. Communication Strategies

Communication Document	Communication Target	Distribution
Complete report with appendices (75 pages)	• Training and education staff • Safety and health staff • Intact team manager	Distributed and discussed in a special meeting
Executive summary (8 pages)	• Senior management in the business units • Senior corporate management	Distributed and discussed in routine meeting
General interest overview and summary without the actual ROI calculation (10 pages)	• Program participants	Mailed with letter
Brochure highlighting program, objectives, and specific results	• Prospective team leaders	Included with other program descriptions

QUESTIONS FOR DISCUSSION

1. How can management involvement be designed into the program? What tools and resources are needed to accomplish this?
2. What criteria should be established to set up the control groups so that the groups are matched appropriately?
3. Identify the major issues and topics planned for the follow-up questionnaire to be administered six months after the program. Include questions to capture the impact of the program on participants and the group.
4. What response rate would you expect from the questionnaire and how can it be improved?
5. What are the total monetary benefits for the program?
6. What is the total cost of the program?
7. What is the return on investment?
8. How could the results be communicated to various groups?
9. Should this study influence policies and practices?

ABOUT THE AUTHORS

Jack J. Phillips, PhD, is chairman of the ROI Institute and a world-renowned expert on measurement and evaluation. Phillips provides consulting services for Fortune 500 companies and workshops for major conference providers worldwide. Phillips is also the author or editor of more than 75 books and more than 100 articles.

Patti P. Phillips, PhD, is an internationally recognized author, consultant, and president and CEO of the ROI Institute. Phillips provides consulting services to organizations worldwide. She helps organizations build capacity in the ROI Methodology by facilitating the ROI certification process and teaching the ROI Methodology through workshops and graduate-level courses.

10

Organizational Change

Measuring the Impact of an Outcome-Based Service Model as a Strategic Planning and Capacity-Building Tool

Holly Burkett, PhD, SPHR, CPT

This case was prepared to serve as a basis for discussion rather than to illustrate either effective or ineffective administrative and management practices. All names, dates, places, and organizations have been disguised at the request of the author(s) or organization.

Abstract

This case study describes both the change process and the evaluation framework used to integrate an outcome-based service model for services provided by a bi-state primary care association for federally supported health clinics. Strategic goals for implementing a results-based service approach included increasing the capacity and sustainability of community health centers to provide high-quality primary and preventive healthcare to patients who might not otherwise have access to it, especially given the increasing number of uninsured. Evaluation results showed a positive link between the organization's implementation of a results-based service model and intended process, program, and service outcomes. Multiple change issues associated with introducing the new service strategy and model into existing functions are discussed, along with implications and recommendations for HR and OD practice.

PURPOSE

Much of the future of a grant or donor-funded association depends upon its ability to demonstrate the effective use of outcome criteria when making decisions about program and service delivery priorities. An evaluation framework is needed to provide understanding about the extent to which grantees are making progress toward stated goals, objectives, and desired outcomes for the individuals or causes they serve. Showing the economic impact of grant or donor-funded programs provides focus when deciding whether to continue or discontinue community, state, or federal resource allocation. In general, evaluation data can also provide important evidence about how community development efforts have fostered knowledge-sharing, forged partnerships, and built individual, organizational, and community capacity.

PROGRAM BACKGROUND AND ORGANIZATIONAL CONTEXT

The Community Health Care Association of the Dakotas (CHAD) is the bi-state primary care association for federally supported health clinics in North and South Dakota. CHAD's membership includes 11 health clinics, four in North Dakota and seven in South Dakota. As the primary care association for two rural, frontier states with widely disbursed populations, CHAD serves a community health clinic (CHC) network through consultation, technical assistance, training, resource development, financial management, and human resource advocacy for the purpose of increasing capacity and sustainability of CHCs. In general, community health centers play a vital role in providing high-quality primary and preventive healthcare to patients who might not otherwise have access to it, especially given the increasing number of uninsured Americans. Federally qualified health centers, also known as community health centers, make up the largest national network of primary care providers. According to Michelle Proser, director of research at the National Association of Community Health Centers (NACHC), "Many patients that would not have access to primary care may end up in the emergency room for services that could have been provided in a primary care setting." This is true not only in urban areas, but also in rural ones, where Proser says half of community health centers, like CHAD, are located. Community health centers, therefore, reduce the number of visits to emergency departments and hospitals; overall, they generate $24 billion in annual savings by saving an average of $1,263 per patient, per year (CHAD, 2010).

OPPORTUNITY

CHAD's mission is to lead the Dakotas in quality primary healthcare through public policy and community driven health services. Its vision is to be recognized and valued for its network of services and expertise that facilitates the missions of "safety net provider" CHC members. An expansion of health clinics in the Dakotas has created a demand for CHAD to provide its members with more diversified and compliance-oriented training and technical assistance services. In light of increased demands for utility and efficiency and a political climate characterized by ongoing resource constraints, the board of directors established strategic priorities around determining the return on investment for "Partnership and Collaboration Activities." Specifically, the strategic plan called upon CHAD's leadership to:

1. Identify the full cost of resource development (programs and services).
2. Make optimum use of resources, including time, money, access to people, equipment, materials, methods, and processes.
3. Assess measures of success with member utilization and satisfaction with CHAD's technical support, educational services, resources, and products.
4. Assess usefulness of the products as translated by use of the information, service, or product to increase healthcare access, quality of care, and CHC capacity.
5. Enhance methods for collecting, organizing, and presenting data about agency outcomes.
6. Focus CHAD efforts on those areas or processes with the highest potential for payoff.
7. Utilize outcome data to better meet member needs.

The key objective was to create a model to determine the payback of staff time and resources regarding CHAD's involvement in state and local communities, task forces, and work groups. And the expected outcome was that CHAD will have a tool by which to measure the efficiency and effectiveness of its partnership and collaboration efforts.

Specific stakeholders and project partners included the agency's CEO, the deputy director, manager of data services, manager of marketing and communication, and four specialists representing such functions as counsel and risk management, financial services, clinical quality, and human resources, respectively. In addition, select CHC members were invited to partner with CHAD in this project and were instrumental in field testing data collection instruments and providing customer/client feedback through an impact questionnaire.

AN OUTCOME-BASED SERVICE MODEL

Providing innovative, outcome-based educational processes, teaching methods, and instructional technologies are a significant aspect of CHAD's consultation, technical assistance, training, and resource work. This work supports regional, state, and local healthcare providers with administrative and clinical recruitment, retention, and professional development. In the context of this research, the appropriate use of outcome-based measures were deemed critical in order to ensure that CHAD's "suite" of educational and technical assistance services were designed, delivered, and monitored to:

- Ensure access to primary, high-quality healthcare.

- Increase capacity of community health center (CHC) members to achieve desired results.
- Make optimum use of CHAD and CHC resources, including time, money, access to people, equipment, materials, methods, and processes.

To address those needs, CHAD commissioned an evaluation consultant to assist in developing an outcome-based approach to measure the efficiency and effectiveness of CHAD's partnership and collaboration activities. The ROI Methodology (Phillips and Phillips, 2007) was selected by CHAD as the evaluation framework and results-based service model for this project. As shown in Figure 10-1, the ROI process expands upon Kirkpatrick's (1974) four-level framework for categorizing evaluation data (reaction, learning, behavior, and results) to incorporate a fifth level of evaluation, which serves to capture the financial impact or return on investment (ROI) of programs. The ROI process model also includes techniques for isolating the effects of a program and for capturing a sixth data measure: intangible benefits.

FIGURE 10-1. Evaluation Framework

Evaluation Levels	Measurement Focus
Level 1 Reaction & Planned Action	Measures participant satisfaction with the program or solution and captures planned actions
Level 2 Learning	Measures changes in knowledge, skills, and attitudes
Level 3 Application	Measures changes in on-the-job behavior
Level 4 Business Impact	Measures changes in business impact variables
Level 5 Return on Investment	Compares program benefits to the costs

DEVELOPING AN OUTCOME-BASED SERVICE MODEL

In general, outcome-based evaluation models assess the short- and long-term results of a project and seek to measure the changes brought about by the project. An outcome evaluation process examines outcomes at multiple levels of the project and helps stakeholders address such questions as: *What are the critical outcomes you are trying to achieve? What impact is the project having on its clients, its staff, its umbrella organization, and its community? What unexpected impact has the project had?*

The Logic Model Approach

An important first step in implementing any outcome-based service strategy is to help program staff and key stakeholders think through the different levels of program outcomes, and understand the importance of starting with individual client/participant outcomes rather than program or systems goals. When evaluating the impacts of more complex system change and comprehensive community initiatives, an evolutionary, flexible approach is needed because ultimate outcomes may not be seen for many years and many of the desired outcomes are difficult to measure using traditional evaluation methods. To that end, CHAD staff and the researcher worked together to develop and document key interim outcomes for tracking the progress of initiatives and for improved understanding about how they lead to the desired long-term outcomes. One effective method for charting progress toward interim and long-term outcomes is through the development and use of a program logic model. A logic model links outcomes (both short- and long-term) with program activities and processes and provides a road map of how desired outcomes are achieved.

In this effort, the logic model approach had several benefits. First, it helped staff stay focused on the changes needed to transition services from an output-based to an outcome-based model; it showed a visual connection between interim and long-term outcomes; it graphically linked CHAD activities, services, and processes to distinct levels of outcomes; and it kept underlying assumptions at the forefront. It was also an effective approach for identifying intangible outcomes (such as increased community participation) or long-term outcomes that would not be achieved for several years. Finally, the actual process of developing the logic model provided a focal point for discussion that facilitated clear thinking around program gaps and opportunities for improvement, as well as a sense of ownership among CHAD stakeholders. As shown in Figure 10-2, this logic model helped illustrate the relationship between activities, outputs, and outcomes at multiple levels.

Each level of evaluation provides important, stand-alone data. Reported together, the five-level ROI framework gives data that tell the complete story of a solution's success or failure. A sixth measure includes capturing data about intangible benefits, which are those measures not converted to monetary value.

PROJECT SCOPE AND PLAN

Based upon strategic imperatives from CHAD's executive board and strategic planning directives, stakeholders defined key objectives of this change effort as follows:

- Implement a results-based evaluation model to determine optimal use of CHAD resources—focus CHAD efforts on those areas that display the highest potential for payoff.

FIGURE 10-2. Logic Model Framework Defining Levels of Outcomes

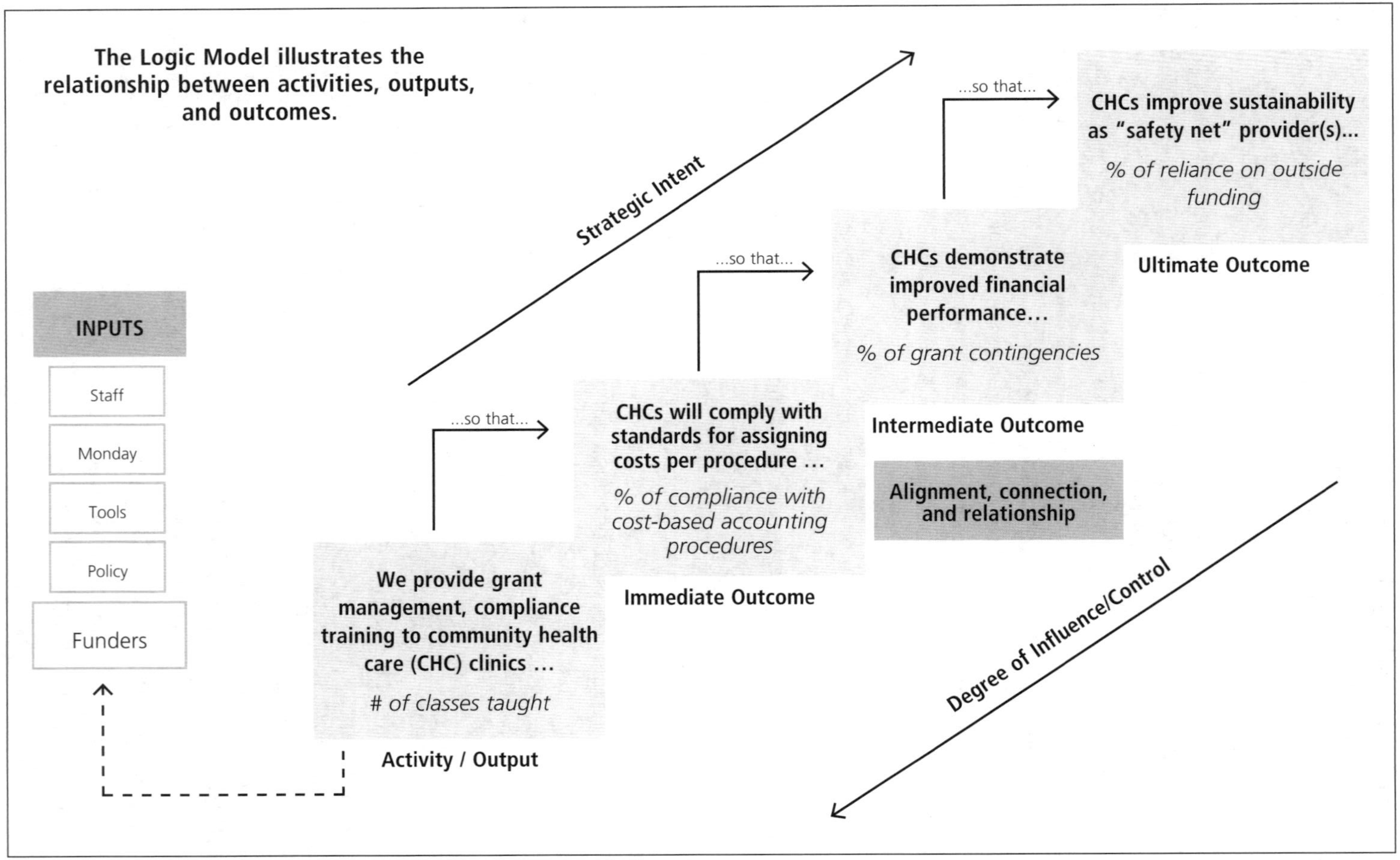

- Assess measures of success with members' satisfaction and members' utilization of CHAD's technical support, educational services, products, and resources.
- Enhance methods for collecting, organizing, and presenting data about CHC outcomes.
- Utilize outcome data to better meet member needs.

In selecting a pilot initiative for introducing an outcome-based measurement process, a comprehensive training project, known as OC3, was chosen. This project represented a series or "suite" of user groups, compliance-oriented trainings for CHC members around such critical issues as: documentation and record retention, cost-based charge scheduling, clinical quality, performance review, and risk management. Training curriculum was a core component of CHAD's efforts to assist CHCs with compliance issues related to regulations from the Uniform Data System (UDS). Specifically, the UDS is an annual reporting system used by all federally funded health centers to report data on utilization, patient demographics, insurance status, managed care, prenatal care and birth outcomes, diagnoses, and financing. UDS assists with program management, policy development, and overall accounting for the programs. It is maintained by the Bureau of Primary Health Care Office of Data, Evaluation, Analysis, and Research, but is also available at NACHC.

TARGET GROUP POPULATION AND PREPARATION

The target groups for the OC3 training included CHC members representing such roles as chief financial officers, directors of finance, office managers, nursing managers, human resource managers, and executive directors. CHAD's executive director, deputy director, and program staff worked with the researcher to purposely select OC3 training participants for the pilot study. Criteria included those participants who:

- could successfully represent multiple service providers and the diverse community perspectives within the CHC member network
- had utilized CHADs TA services on at least four occasions within the last 12 months
- were perceived as active leaders in network task forces, network meetings, and network events
- were perceived as influential change agents within their respective health centers
- were able to provide expert feedback about the value of compliance readiness training to CHAD staff for continuous improvement and action planning purposes.

To invite their participation in this evaluation effort, CHAD staff placed individual phone calls to the select representatives to explain the purpose and importance of the project. All who were invited agreed to participate voluntarily. A letter and email follow-up was then generated by the CHAD's deputy director and the evaluation consultant to invite participants to one of two scheduled 60-minute, semi-structured virtual meetings; during which, the purpose of the outcome-based service model for CHAD's TA initiatives was once again reviewed and participants' role and responsibilities in the data collection process was explained. In initial meetings, participants were advised that they would be invited to provide written feedback, through an impact questionnaire, about the extent to which the OC3 training achieved its intended objectives.

In scheduled follow-up meetings with participants, post-training, special attention was given to orienting individuals to the impact questionnaire, especially around how to define the organizational impact of any applied skills from the OC3 training. Specific CHC examples were provided by CHAD's specialists. Participants were assured that they would receive evaluation results and that individual responses would be part of an aggregate report to the executive board about the effectiveness of the outcome-based service approach.

Evaluation Planning Procedures

Evaluation planning includes working with respective specialists in documentation and record retention, cost-based charge scheduling, clinical quality, performance review, and risk management functional areas to define program objectives across the multiple levels of impact, including reaction, learning, application, and impact objectives (per the five-level framework). For example, the first type of data—participants' *reaction*—is measured on almost all programs, usually with questionnaires and surveys. *Learning* measurements check to ensure that participants gain new skills, absorb knowledge, and grasp how to make the program successful. Measuring *application* determines if participants are applying desired program behaviors successfully back on their work site. Measuring *impact* focuses on actual consequences achieved for the business or organization, as a direct result of participants' applied behaviors and program involvement. Typical measures include output, quality, costs, time, and employee satisfaction. *ROI* is the ultimate level of evaluation, where the impact measures are converted to monetary benefits and compared with the costs. ROI is usually expressed as a percentage as follows:

$$\text{ROI (\%)} = \frac{\text{Net Program Benefits}}{\text{Program Costs}} \times 100 = \%\text{ROI}$$

Using this framework, Figure 10-3 illustrates how evaluation planning efforts led to defined learning and application objectives for one core component of the OC3 curriculum. As shown, this data collection plan was developed to document expected outcomes and to describe what outcome and activity data would be collected, how it

FIGURE 10-3. Sample Data Collection

Plan: Cost-Based Calculations Training

Objectives	Indicators	Enablers/Barriers	Data Collection		
			Methods	Source	Timing
• Identify the formula for calculating average cost per visit for medical services. • Transform formula into a charge schedule for medical services.	• Participants will identify four ways of assessing costs. • Participants will utilize the calculated, average Relative Value Unit (RVU) to assign costs per procedure.	Enablers: • Technical assistance • Funding requirements Barriers: • Not enough time to apply learning • Limited support from supervisor	• Large group discussion ◦ Pre/post-activity ◦ Skill practice observation • Record review (audits) ◦ Impact questionnaire ◦ User group meetings	• Participants ◦ Directors • Participants ◦ Clinic data ◦ Directors ◦ Training specialists	• During Training • 30, 60 days after training

would be collected, when it would be collected, and who was responsible for collecting it. This approach helped ensure a common language for defining results as well as a shared ownership for achieving results.

It should be noted that early planning involved establishing methods to pursue evaluation at Level 5, the ROI level. However, during the data collection and analysis phase, the staff ultimately determined that they were satisfied with impact data and did not have the resources or desire to determine fully loaded costs associated with the project in order to conduct a benefit-cost analysis comparing program costs to program benefits. This resource constraint was largely due to complicated and unexpected personal issues with one of the key project sponsors, which greatly affected data collection efforts.

Data Gathering Methods

Data collection methods included administering an impact questionnaire; facilitating semi-structured, qualitative interview sessions with stakeholders; and review of extant historical data. The impact questionnaire, to be distributed 60 days post-training, was reviewed by six content experts to ensure face validity, clarify ambiguous or unclear instructions, and assess relevance of questionnaire items to research objectives. It was also field-tested with a select group of five participants, prior to implementation, and refined based upon field input.

Data Analysis Procedures

The ROI Methodology employs specific data analysis procedures. This includes methods of isolating the program's effect and then converting improvement data to monetary value. The isolation step is essential to data analysis because many factors will influence outcome data. Data gathered in this step pinpoints the amount of improvement directly related to the project under review, resulting in increased accuracy and credibility of ROI calculations. In this study, participant estimates were used to place a value on each unit of measure connected with the OC3 initiative. The effectiveness of this approach rests on the assumption that participants are capable of estimating how much a performance improvement measure is related to application of learned skills and knowledge. In this case, participants were considered credible sources of data to senior management. If no improvement data was available from a specific source, the assumption is that little or no improvement occurred. Sample impact questions showing use of estimates included:

- *What specific actions did you apply based upon what you have learned?*
- *What specific business unit of measure was influenced by your actions?*
- *As a result of these changes, please estimate the monetary benefits to your work unit over a one month period.*
- *What is the basis for your estimate?*

- *What level of confidence, expressed as a percentage, do you place on the above estimate? (100% = Certainty and 0% = No Confidence)*
- *What other factors, besides training or technical assistance, may contribute to benefits associated with your applied skills or knowledge?*
- *Other factor ________%*

Finally, data analysis and reporting also included analysis of barriers and enablers to participants' application of knowledge and skills, as well as intangible benefits and recommendations for program improvement.

EVALUATION RESULTS

Level 1: Reaction, Planned Action

Results were successful with 100 percent of participants indicating that OC3 participation represented a worthwhile investment of time. All of the participants identified planned actions they would take as a result of participation and 100 percent stated that they would recommend the OC3 training to others. Program content was described as *very relevant* by 38 percent and *mostly relevant* by 54 percent.

Level 2: Learning

Learning results were measured using a five-point scale with 1 being "no success" and 5 being "completely successful." Key learning gains included enhanced knowledge or awareness about:

- methods for collecting data about agency outcomes (such as internal control systems, risk liability management, job performance, and performance appraisal systems)
- methods for organizing data about agency outcomes (such as medical record review, HIPAA information, UDS reporting, front desk fiscal monitoring, tracking of receipts)
- focusing on data relevant to client outcomes (such as reviewing expenditures and accounts, medical releases, retention of documents)
- accessing partner networks.

Level 3: Application

The impact questionnaire addressed such fundamental questions as:

- *What actions were taken as a result of key learnings from OC3 training participation?*
- *What behaviors, skills, resources, or materials were used most frequently?*
- *What on-the-job improvements were realized with applied knowledge/skill from OC3 training?*

An example of application questions focused upon one element of the OC3 training "suite" is shown in Figure 10-4.

FIGURE 10-4. Sample Application Questions in Impact Questionnaire

Scale	1	2	3	4	5
Extent of Use in Last 60 Days	No Extent	Some Extent	Moderate Extent	Significant Extent	Very Significant Extent

Program Objective(s)	Frequency	Effectiveness
a. Apply RVU formula for calculating costs per visit for medical services	1 2 3 4 5	1 2 3 4 5
b. Transform RVU formula into appropriate charge schedule for medical services	1 2 3 4 5	1 2 3 4 5
c. Establish monthly tracking system to monitor compliance with fee scheduling criteria	1 2 3 4 5	1 2 3 4 5
d. Develop internal safeguards to minimize the risk of fraud	1 2 3 4 5	1 2 3 4 5
e. Complete a "Medical Record Completion Review"	1 2 3 4 5	1 2 3 4 5
f. Utilize a three-file record keeping system for improved human resource record keeping and retention	1 2 3 4 5	1 2 3 4 5

Overall, the most frequently used behaviors, skills, resources, and materials included financial management tools, document control and medical record management tools, human resource materials for performance appraisals, and risk management resources. Barriers and enablers to participants' application of learned knowledge and skills were also captured in the impact questionnaire. The most frequently reported barrier to implementing OC3 training knowledge or skills was "lack of time."

Level 4: Impact

Impact data were collected in the impact questionnaire by asking participants about the result of their actions upon specific work measures, perceived cost benefits of applied behaviors upon defined work measures, and intangible benefits of applied knowledge and skills. For example, the impact questionnaire captured impact data by asking in Q8: *"Please indicate the extent to which utilization of skills, material, or resources gained from participation in the CHAD Training(s) has influenced the following areas of business effectiveness within your department or your workplace."* These business areas included:

- cost control, cost conversions, and cost-based fees
- operational performance
- quality of services
- customer response
- customer satisfaction
- performance management
- ability to meet Health Center program requirements
- risk management
- ability to meet grant requirements
- ability to improve statewide visibility of the Community Health Centers.

The areas of business effectiveness most positively influenced by OC3 training participation included risk management (31 percent *significant influence*), ability to meet grant requirements (23 percent *significant influence*), customer satisfaction (15 percent *significant influence*), and ability to meet Health Center requirements (15 percent *significant influence*). Cost control was reported at 9 percent *very significant influence* and operational performance at 8 percent *very significant influence.*

Since many factors influence business or performance improvement, additional impact data were captured to isolate the effect of these other influences. Specifically, Question 9 asked: *"Of the following, what specific work improvements (if any) can be attributed to your participation in the CHAD OC3 Training(s). Consider how any improvement in business processes or daily operations have actually helped your work unit or your workplace. Check all that apply"*:

- improved time savings
- improved compliance with funding requirements
- less rework or duplication of efforts
- reduced error rates
- improved quality of care
- improved collaboration with partners
- improved decision making due to better planning and analysis
- improved reporting and billing capabilities
- other.

Data Conversion

Once the other factors that influenced business or performance improvement were isolated, any available Level 4 Impact data were converted to monetary value. Table 10-1 provides a sample of the monetary values that seven participants assigned to the category of "*Improved compliance with funding requirements*." Not all survey respondents supplied this data due to conflicting messages about the need for this information. In general, business benefits that translated to cost savings were described as those related to rework or lost labor time associated with one incident of a grant noncompliance (Column A). In accordance with Phillips' ROI process, these values were then adjusted to account for potential error (Column B) and other influences besides OC3 training that may have contributed to this benefit (Column C). Next, the adjusted values (Column D) were totaled for all participants who supplied this data.

The data conversion process was conservative, with the assumption that unresponsive participants had realized no improvement and that cost benefits were factored on an annualized basis only. These values (and others) would typically then be used as cost-benefit data and compared to program costs in the final ROI analysis and calculation. However, as previously stated, it was ultimately determined by the staff that ROI calculations were not going to be captured for this pilot effort.

Intangible Benefits

Intangible benefits are those benefits linked directly to the program, but not converted to monetary value. Intangible benefits from this study that were of most interest to stakeholders included:

- increased knowledge of health center operational and business issues
- better understanding of medical records release issues
- reduced time in policy development and purchasing resource materials
- ability to receive timely, relevant information without losing travel time
- increased insight on by-law requirements
- increased ability to analyze front desk cash control procedures
- improved ability to complete a healthcare plan showing achievable, measurable goal statements.

Additional areas of intangible benefits included participants' reports of improved *personal effectiveness* (Question 7) in such areas as: organizing and prioritizing work, utilizing CHAD resources, analyzing continuous improvement opportunities, and implementing continuous improvement processes to enhance operational performance.

TABLE 10-1. Sample Monetary Values

Participant #	Unit of Measure	Basis of Estimate	Improvement Value (A) x	Confidence Estimate (B) x	% Change Due to Program (C) x	Adjusted Cost Benefit Attributed to Training = D
1.	Non-compliance incident	NOGA Report	$450.00 per incident	30%	40%	$54.00
2.	Non-compliance incident	NOGA Report	$1,690.00 per incident	98%	80%	$1,324.96
3.	Non-compliance incident	NOGA Report	$375.00 per incident	80%	80%	$240.00
4.	Non-compliance incident	NOGA Report	$350.00 per incident	90%	80%	$252.00
5.	Non-compliance incident	NOGA Report	$1,200.00	60%	60%	$432.00
6.	Non-compliance incident	NOGA Report	$250.00	80%	100%	$200.00
7.	Non-compliance incident	NOGA Report	$6,500.00*	30%	30%	$585.00
Total Estimated Cost Benefit for Grant Incident Prevention/ Avoidance *Directly* Attributable to Training					**$3,087.96**	

* While the ROI Methodology™ would typically exclude extreme data items, subject matter experts determined that this individuals' basis of estimate was credible and reflected experience with the historical costs associated with noncompliance.

COMMUNICATING RESULTS

Upon completion of the pilot study, a one-hour briefing, with corresponding PowerPoint slides and an executive summary report (Figure 10-5), was presented to executive sponsors, participants, and executive board members. Results were also communicated to the CHC member network on the agency's website. In addition, at a subsequent regional conference held for CHC service providers, CHAD's deputy director and the evaluation consultant presented concurrent conference sessions in which the ROI Methodology was introduced as CHAD's newly adopted, outcome-based

FIGURE 10-5. Executive Summary

Streamlined Impact Report for OC3 Pilot Project

Project Objectives:

- Implement a results-based evaluation model to determine optimal use of CHAD resources—focus CHAD efforts on those areas that display the highest potential for payoff.
- Assess measures of success with members' satisfaction and members' utilization of CHAD's technical support, educational services, products, and resources.
- Enhance methods for collecting, organizing, and presenting data about CHC outcomes.
- Utilize outcome data to better meet member needs.
- Assess the change management issues associated with the transition from an output-based service focus to a results-based service focus.

→ **Levels of Evaluation** →

Satisfaction, Reaction, Planned Action Results	Learning Results	Application Results (Use of Learned Skills, Knowledge On-the-Job)	Business Impact (Specific Work Improvements Directly Attributable to Training)	Intangible Benefits
I would recommend this training to others: 100% Program content was relevant to my daily job: • 69% Mostly Relevant • 15% Very Relevant	Confidence in using learned skills, knowledge: • 54% Very Confident	Extent of use with learned skills, knowledge: • 45% Very Frequent • 15% Consistent Use Utilizing CHAD resources: • 23% Significant Influence	Cost control, cost conversions: • 9% Very Significant Influence Operational Performance: • 8% Very Significant Influence	Increased knowledge of Health Center operational and business issues Better understanding of medical records release issues

Resource material was relevant to my daily job: • 54% Mostly Relevant • 38% Very Relevant CHAD services, training(s) represented a good investment for my agency: 100% The evaluation project represented a good investment for CHAD: 100%	Effectiveness in using learned skills, knowledge: • 45% Very Frequent • 15% Very Effective	Implementing continuous improvement opportunities to enhance operational performance: • 23% Significant Influence Implement improvements in policies, procedures around medical releases: • 45% Mostly Successful Skills, materials, resources used most often (sample): • HIPAA • UDS Manuals • UDS Reporting • Front desk cost effectiveness • Medical record releases • Regular reviewing of expenditures, accounts • Controls for recording of receipts	Risk Management: • 31% Significant Influence Customer Satisfaction: • 15% Significant Influence Other: • 38% Improved Collaboration • 31% Improved Time Savings • 23% Improved Compliance • 23% Improved Decision Making Estimated monetary benefits from incident (NOGA) prevention: $3,087.96 per incident Influence on CHAD's operational performance: • 33% Very Significant Influence on Perceived Proactivity	Reduced time in policy development and purchasing resource materials Ability to receive timely, relevant information without losing travel time Increased insight on by-law requirements Increased ability to analyze front desk cash control procedures Improved ability to complete a healthcare plan showing achievable, measurable goal statements

approach for meeting strategic healthcare imperatives on a national level and CHC member needs on a regional level.

In general, reported results emphasized practical, tangible benefits associated with implementing the ROI process as an outcome-based service model, including its perceived contribution to targeted TA objectives of enhancing service capacity and sustainability of the CHCs, and enhancing perceptions of CHAD's partnership and collaborative services as being proactive, timely, relevant, quality-oriented, and results-focused. Specifically, findings from the preliminary pilot study suggest that project objectives and desired changes were successfully achieved. For example, participants who applied OC3 knowledge and skills to their respective health centers reported that they significantly affected targeted measures of improved service delivery, improved ability to meet grant requirements, improved quality of patient satisfaction, and improved ability to meet Health Center requirements. Stakeholders were particularly pleased with results showing that 100 percent of participants perceived the evaluation pilot to be a good investment for CHAD.

Upon completion of the pilot evaluation project, CHAD incorporated the ROI Methodology as an outcome-based service model by integrating it into its subsequent strategic plan, per the following:

- Facilitate ROI evaluation process on other CHAD activities.
- Facilitate impact surveys on all training opportunities offered by CHAD.
- Facilitate ROI evaluation on business development activities, PCA grant activities, and strategic planning activities.
- Incorporate ROI process in all future planning efforts.

CHANGE MANAGEMENT IMPLICATIONS

In a 2009 report for the IBM Center for the Business of Government, Callahan and Kloby state that, "Implementing a results-oriented focus represents a fundamental shift in the way the public sector does business—a fundamental shift in the nature of thinking, acting, and managing that moves away from a focus on process and regulation to a focus on outcomes and results." Results from this evaluation project confirm existing studies showing that internalizing a comprehensive business process—such as a results-based evaluation process—into a service strategy or function is a complex undertaking that requires fundamental, cultural changes to policies, processes, and programs across all organizational levels (Kusek and Rist, 2004). For example, implementation of an outcome-based service model represents a transformational, continuous change process because it: 1) requires practitioners to conceive broad-based, new methods of data collection, data analysis, data retrieval, and data reporting, among other duties; and

2) introduces evaluation procedures, routines, processes, or systems that require increased organizational accountability and transparency with respect to performance results.

Specific change responses and emotional concerns often associated with transitioning from outputs to outcomes include fear of accountability, fear about learning new evaluation techniques, and fear of consequences about how performance data will be used, among others (Phillips et al., 2006; Preskill and Russ-Eft, 2005). Given these and other change issues typical of any large-scale change effort, the following aspects of change planning were integrated as an iterative process during CHAD's early adoption and pilot implementation of the ROI process as an outcome-based service model.

- **Transition planning:** Included development of: policy and purpose statements, preliminary infrastructures (such as database structures) to support results-based efforts, data collection protocol and instruments, implementation project plans and action item review, and updating of specialist roles and responsibilities to include accountabilities for the use of outcome-based measures in monitoring personal and job effectiveness.
- **Capacity building:** Included formal and informal continuing training, education, and professional development for CHAD staff around the concept, practice, and operating standards associated with ROI process implementation. Evaluation capacity building activities ranged from structured, one- to two-day intensive skill building workshops, to individual coaching sessions around curriculum design, to frequent face-to-face and telephone consultations with project sponsors around how to best support and reinforce outcome-based service approaches across process, program, and organizational levels.

SUMMARY AND FOLLOW UP

Despite early success with pilot project implementation, subsequent follow-up assessment—more than one year later—shows that attempts to fully integrate the outcome-based evaluation framework as a standardized service strategy and business process for CHAD's TA function have encountered many predictable, and unpredictable, challenges and barriers. These include volatile changes in the healthcare and economic environments as well as dynamic changes in the organization related to staff resource constraints and conflicting priorities around allocation of resources, particularly those dedicated to evaluation of service outcomes. These findings support existing studies showing that volatile change environments and conflicting resource demands can negate real and anticipated benefits of any process improvement effort (Herold, Fedor, and Caldwell, 2007; Mourier and Smith, 2001).

IMPLICATIONS FOR PRACTICE

By 2015, the National Association of Community Health Centers estimates that health centers will double their current capacity to 40 million patients. Yet recent budgets passed by the U.S. House reportedly call for a $1.3 billion cut to community health centers nationwide. Given increased demands to double capacity while also bringing down costs, more and more funding sources will be requiring evidence of demonstrable results to justify continued investments. This case study illustrates how an outcome-based service model can be used as a continuous improvement tool by which to measure efficiency and effectiveness of federally funded community partnership and collaboration services. Effective adaptability and utilization of an outcome-based evaluation framework ensures that decision makers will have a durable, credible process for helping to focus on programs or services that provide the most value returned for resources invested. Establishing a collaborative approach to defining and evaluating service outcomes was also found to be beneficial to partners involved in this effort.

While there are common elements (such as collaboration) that can lead to successful implementation of a comprehensive, results-based evaluation process system like the ROI Methodology, sustaining the process and keeping it on track is an aspect of implementation that is often overlooked and underestimated (Burkett, 2008; Phillips et al., 2006). Organizations that seek to implement outcome-based evaluation processes without full assessment of real and potential change factors, will risk a decline in productivity, a reduction in employee engagement and organizational commitment, and a decrease in profitability. These risks will increase exponentially as the environment in which the results-based process is to be embedded becomes more turbulent, resulting in sponsors' attention and evaluation resources being progressively diverted due to conflicting and overlapping change priorities. To that end, the more planned change strategies are integrated with complex organizational development initiatives, the more sustainable the implementation is likely to be (Anderson and Anderson, 2001; Appleby and Tempest, 2006).

While there is no shortage of literature about how to manage change and develop change capacity, attending to change issues remains an elusive leadership practice. Change management capacity and capability vary greatly from one organization to another. Even organizations that experience constant change do not necessarily have this as a core competency. Research shows that leaders and followers agree that a leader's capacity to assess change progress during implementation, and to sustain efforts post-implementation, is a prevalent area of limitation that impedes change success and exhausts critical resources (Herold et al., 2007). While there is no best way to sustain an outcome-based service model in the face of omnipresent change, recognition of the change issues associated with sustainable implementation can help organizations target interventions and allocate resources to those leverage points that will have the greatest influence on its change adaptability and utility.

REFERENCES

Amble, B. (2010, January). "Good Change Management a Key Driver of Success." *Management-Issues*. Retrieved January 7, 2010 from http://www.management-issues.com/2010/1/26/research/good-change-management-a-key-driver-of-success.asp.

Anderson, D., and L. Anderson. (2001). *Beyond Change Management: Advanced Strategies for Today's Transformational Leaders*. San Francisco: Wiley.

Appleby, H., and S. Tempest. (2006, October). "Using Change Management Theory to Implement the International Classification of Functioning, Disability, and Health (ICF) in Clinical Practice." *British Journal of Occupational Therapy*, 69(10): 1-4.

Burkett, H. (2008). "Transition Planning Steps for Building and Sustaining a Results-based Learning Focus." In Gargiulo, T., A. Pangarkar, and T. Kirkwood (eds.), *The Trainer's Portable Mentor*. San Francisco: Pfeiffer.

Callahan, K., and K. Kloby. (2009). *Moving Towards Outcome-Oriented Performance Measurement Systems*. Washington, D.C.: The IBM Center for the Business of Government.

Chakravorty, S.S. (2010, January 22). "Where Process Improvement Projects Go Wrong." *MIT Sloan Management Review*. Retrieved April 12, 2010 from http://sloanreview.mit.edu/executive-adviser/articles/2010/1/5214/where-process-improvement-projects-go-wrong.

French, W., and S. Bell. (1995). *Organization Development: Behavioral Science Interventions for Organizational Improvement*, (5th edition). Englewood Cliffs, NJ: Prentice-Hall.

Herold, D.M., D.F. Fedor, and S.D. Caldwell. (2007). "Beyond Change Management: A Multi-level Investigation of Contextual and Personal Influences on Employees' Commitment to Change." *Journal of Applied Psychology*. 92: 942-951.

Kusek, J.Z., and R.C. Rist. (2004). *Ten Steps to a Results-Based Monitoring and Evaluation System: A Handbook for Development Practitioners*. Washington, D.C.: The World Bank.

Mourier, P., & M. Smith. (2001). *Conquering Organizational Change*. Atlanta, GA: CEP Press.

Phillips, J.J., P. Phillips, R. Stone, and H. Burkett. (2006). *The ROI Fieldbook: Strategies for Implementing ROI in HR and Training*. St. Louis: Elsevier/Butterworth-Heinemann.

Preskill, H., & D. Russ-Eft. (2005). *Building Evaluation Capacity*. Thousand Oaks, CA: Sage.

ABOUT THE AUTHOR

Holly Burkett, PhD, SPHR, CPT is Principal of Evaluation Works in Davis, California. A certified ROI professional, she has more than 20 years' experience assisting public and private sector clients design and implement outcome-based systems and measures of program effectiveness. Recognized as an evaluation expert with the U.S. Department of Health and Human Services, Health Resources, and Services Administration (HRSA) Office of Performance Review (OPR), she is a frequent conference presenter, workshop leader, and author on performance measurement issues. Sample clients include: The International Union Against Tuberculosis and Lung Disease; Apple Computer; California Public Employees Retirement System (CalPERS); and the Kansas Association of the Medically Underserved (KAMU). Former editor of ISPI's acclaimed *Performance Improvement Journal*, her publications include authoring the "Action Planning" chapter in the *ASTD Handbook of Measuring & Evaluating Training* (2010) and co-authoring *The ROI Fieldbook* (2006) with Jack and Patti Phillips and Ron Stone. She holds a PhD in human capital development and a master's degree in human resources and organization development (HROD) from the University of San Francisco. Holly can be reached at burketth@earthlink.net.

References for Part 1

ASTD Research. (2012). *State of the Industry Report.* Alexandria, VA: ASTD Press.

Bakker, A.B., and W.B. Schaufeli. (February, 2008). "Editorial: Positive Organizational Behavior: Engaged Employees in Flourishing Organizations." *Journal of Organizational Behavior*, 29(2), pp. 147–154.

Balzac, S. (2010). *The McGraw-Hill 36-Hour Course: Organizational Development.* New York: McGraw-Hill.

Beard, M. J., and L. Zuniga. (2006). "Achieving the Right Flavor: A Study of Designing a Cultural Integration Process." *The Psychologist-Manager Journal,* 9(1), pp. 13–25.

Belasco, J. (1990). *Teaching the Elephant to Dance: Empowering Change in Your Organization.* New York: Crown Publishers.

Bennis, W.G. (1969). *Organization Development: Its Nature, Origins, and Prospects.* Boston: Addison-Wesley.

Berson, Y., S. Oreg, and T. Dvir. (July, 2008). "CEO Values, Organizational Culture and Firm Outcomes." *Journal of Organizational Behavior, 29*(5), pp. 615–633.

Bryant, S. (March, 10, 2011). "E-commerce Predicted to Grow by Double-Digits Through 2015," http://www.marketingforecast.com/archives/10413.

Daft, R.L. (1995). *Organizational Theory and Design.* St. Paul: West Publishing.

DuBois, S. (July, 2012). "The Rise of the Chief Culture Officer." *Fortune Magazine*, http://management.fortune.cnn.com/2012/07/30/chief-culture-officers/.

Eddy, E.R., C.P. D'Abate, S.I. Tannenbaum, S. Givens-Skeaton, and G. Robinson. (2006). "Key Characteristics of Effective and Ineffective Developmental Interactions." *Human Resource Development Quarterly*, 17, 59–84.

Ferraro, G. (2009). *Classic Readings in Cultural Anthropology,* 2nd edition. Stamford: Wadsworth Cengage Learning.

Gilbert, I. (2013). *Essential Motivation in the Classroom.* New York: Routledge.

Goffee, R., and G. Jones. (1998). *The Character of a Corporation: How Your Company's Culture Can Make or Break Your Business.* UK: Collins.

Golembiewski and Sun. (1990). "ÓD: Past, Present and Future" (2012), http://creativemovesbpo.weebly.com/5/post/2012/09/od-past-present-and-future-part-1-of-4.html.

Gostick, A. and C. Elton. (2012). *All In: How the Best Managers Create a Culture of Belief and Drive Big Results.* New York: Free Press.

Harms, P.D., and F. Luthans. (May, 2012). "Measuring Implicit Psychological Constructs in Organizational Behavior: An Example Using Psychology Capital." *Journal of Organizational Behavior, 33*(4), pp. 589–594.

Horestay, D. (August, 1998). "Cracking the Whip." *Government Executive,* http://www.govexec.com/magazine/1998/08/cracking-the-whip/5789/.

Judge, T.A., and J.D. Kammeyer-Mueller. (February, 2012). "General and Specific Measures in Organizational Behavior Research: Considerations, Examples, and Recommendations for Researchers." *Journal of Organizational Behavior, 33*(2), pp. 161–174.

Kahnweiler, W. (July, 2010). "Organization Development Success and Failure: A Case Analysis." *Organization Development Journal, 28*(2).

Korten, F., L. De Caluwe, and J. Geurts. (October 21, 2010). "The Future of Organization Development: A Delphi Study Among Dutch Experts." *Journal of Change Management,* http://www.avannistelrooij.nl/website/files/Korten%20ea%20(2010)%20future%20OD%20JCM.pdf.

Kotter, J.P. (2008). *A Sense of Urgency.* Boston: Harvard Business School Publishing.

Kotter, J.P. (1998). "Leading Change: Why Transformation Efforts Fail." *Harvard Business Review on Change.* Boston: Harvard Business School Press.

Kwan, P., and A. Walker. (2004). "Validating the Competing Values Model as a Representation of Organizational Culture Through Inter-Institutional Comparisons." *Organizational Analysis, 12*(1), pp. 21–37.

Lakshminarayanan, S. (2011). "Organizational Behavior and Work: A Critical Introduction." *Organization Management Journal, 8*(2), pp. 132–134.

Lencioni, P. (2012). *The Advantage.* San Francisco: Jossey-Bass.

Marr, B. (November, 2012). "Analytics at Google: Great Example of Data-Driven Decision Making." *Smart Data Collective,* http://smartdatacollective.com/bernardmarr/85871/analytics-google-great-example-data-driven-decision-making.

Merrell, P. (2012). "Effective Change Management: The Simple Truth." *Management Services, 56*(2), pp. 20–23.

Moore, H. (February, 2008). "Sprint Nextel: Officially a Deal From Hell." *Wall Street Journal,* http://blogs.wsj.com/deals/2008/02/28/sprint-nextel-officially-a-deal-from-hell/.

PricewaterhouseCoopers International. (2013). "Dealing With Disruption: Adapting to Survive and Thrive." 16th Annual Global CEO Survey, http://www.pwc.com/gx/en/ceo-survey/2013/assets/pwc-16th-global-ceo-survey_jan-2013.pdf.

Prosci (2012). "Change Management Process and Model," http://www.change-management.com/change-management-process.htm.

Rackham, N. (1988). *Spin Selling.* New York: McGraw-Hill.

Schein, E. (2010). *Organizational Culture and Leadership.* San Francisco: John Wiley & Sons.

Schultz, V. (2003). "The Sanitized Workplace." *Yale Law Journal, 112,* 2061–2194.

Senge, P. (2006). *The Fifth Discipline: The Art and Practice of the Learning Organization.* New York: Doubleday.

Smith, D. (October 19, 2008). "Why Do Most IT Projects Fail? It's Not Because of the Technology." The *Portland Business Journal,* http://www.bizjournals.com/portland/stories/2008/10/20/smallb4.html?page = all.

Smith, M.K. (2001). "Kurt Lewin: Groups, Experiential Learning and Action Research," http://www.infed.org/thinkers/et-lewin.htm (accessed September 9, 2004).

Sullivan, R., B. Rothwell, and C. Worley. (2011). *20th Edition of the Organization Change and Development Competency Effort,* http://c.ymcdn.com/sites/www.odnetwork.org/resource/resmgr/docs/od_competencies.pdf.

Teoh, A. (August/September, 2010). "Why IT Projects Fail." *The Project Manager.*

University of Michigan and RBL Group. (2012). "HR Competencies," http://www.sitemaker.umich.edu/hrcs/executive_summary.

Waclawski, J., and A.H. Church. (2001). *Organization Development: A Data-Driven Approach to Organizational Change.* San Francisco: Jossey-Bass.

Weisbord, M.R. (1978). *Organizational Diagnosis: A Workbook of Theory and Practice.* Wynnewood, PA: Perseus Books.

About the ROI Institute

The ROI Institute, Inc. is the leading resource on research, training, and networking for practitioners of the Phillips ROI Methodology.

With a combined 50 years of experience in measuring and evaluating training, human resources, technology, and quality programs and initiatives, founders and owners Jack J. Phillips, PhD, and Patti P. Phillips, PhD, are the leading experts in return on investment (ROI).

The ROI Institute, founded in 1992, is a service-driven organization that strives to assist professionals in improving their programs and processes through the use of the ROI Methodology. Developed by Jack Phillips, this methodology is a critical tool for measuring and evaluating programs in 18 different applications in more than 60 countries.

The ROI Institute offers a variety of consulting services, learning opportunities, and publications. In addition, it conducts internal research activities for the organization, other enterprises, public sector entities, industries, and interest groups. Together with their team, Jack and Patti Phillips serve private and public sector organizations globally.

BUILD CAPABILITY IN THE ROI METHODOLOGY

The ROI Institute offers a variety of workshops to help you build capability in the ROI Methodology. Among the many workshops offered through the ROI Institute are:

- One-day *Bottomline on ROI* Workshop—Provides the perfect introduction to all levels of measurement, including the most sophisticated level, ROI. Learn the key principles of the Phillips ROI Methodology and determine whether your organization is ready to implement the process.
- Two-day *ROI Competency Building* Workshop—The standard ROI Workshop on measurement and evaluation, this two-day program involves discussion of the ROI Methodology process, including data collection, isolation methods, data conversion, and more.

ROI CERTIFICATION™

The ROI Institute is the only organization offering certification in the ROI Methodology. Through the ROI Certification process, you can build expertise in implementing ROI evaluation and sustaining the measurement and evaluation process in your organization. Receive personalized coaching while conducting an impact study. When competencies in the ROI Methodology have been demonstrated, certification is awarded. There is not another process that provides access to the same level of expertise as our ROI Certification. To date, more than 7,000 individuals have participated in this process.

For more information on these and other workshops, learning opportunities, consulting, and research, please visit us on the web at **www.roiinstitute.net,** or call us at **205.678.8101**.

About the Authors

Patricia Pulliam Phillips, PhD, is an internationally recognized author, consultant, and president and CEO of the ROI Institute, Inc. Phillips provides consulting services to organizations worldwide. She helps organizations build capacity in the ROI Methodology by facilitating the ROI certification process and teaching the ROI Methodology through workshops and graduate-level courses. Phillips has a PhD in international development and a master's degree in public and private management. She is certified in ROI evaluation and has been awarded the designations of Certified Professional in Learning and Performance and Certified Performance Technologist.

Jack J. Phillips, PhD, is chairman of the ROI Institute and a world-renowned expert on measurement and evaluation. Phillips provides consulting services for Fortune 500 companies and workshops for major conference providers worldwide. Phillips is also the author or editor of more than 75 books and more than 100 articles. His work has been featured in the *Wall Street Journal*, *Bloomberg Businessweek*, *Fortune*, and on CNN.

Lizette Zuniga, PhD, brings more than 15 years of experience to the field of human resource development. She specializes in organization development, assessment, leadership development, and measurement and evaluation. Growing up in a Cuban family in the southern U.S., she naturally gravitates toward culture and working with culturally diverse groups. Dr. Zuniga facilitates a variety of organization development methods to achieve bottom-line results. She has assisted organizations in OD interventions, leadership and team development, and learning and development activities, tying the outcomes to tangible business results. Organizational assessment, needs assessment and leadership competency assessment are tools that Dr. Zuniga frequently uses in her work. Dr. Zuniga co-authored the book *Costs and ROI: Evaluating at the Ultimate Level* with Jack Phillips and has published several articles and book chapters. She holds a master's degree in counseling psychology from Georgia State University, Atlanta, Georgia, and a PhD in leadership from Barry University, Miami, Florida. She maintains her license as a mental health counselor in the state of Florida, and is certified as a ROI professional and in Myers Briggs Typology. Lizette volunteers on an advisory committee that is dedicated to help children in Cuba with medical, psychological and/or nutritional needs, with the goal of improving their daily lives, education, and overall well-being. Some of her other interests are travel, cultural films, and reading. She can be reached at lizette.zuniga@icloud.com.

Index

A

Absenteeism, 91
Acquisition costs, 96
Action plan(s)
  adjustments to, 72–73
  collection of, 72
  confidence level for estimates, 71–72
  estimates used in, 71–72
  example of, 70
  feedback, 109
  goal and target setting in, 69
  implementation of, 71
  improvements, 69, 71
  isolating the effects of the intervention, 71
  monetary value placed on improvements, 69, 71
  purpose of, 68
  SMART requirements for, 69
  unit of measure for, 69
Action planning process, 20
Action research, 5, 7, 20
Activity-based initiatives, 32–33
Anonymous questionnaires, 62
Antineau, Lori, 20
Application objectives, 51
Autocratic leadership style, 30

B

Behavior change
  consequences of, 36
  data from, 36
  time allowed for, 76
Behavior change and performance evaluation, 42
Belasco, James, 9
Benefit-cost ratio, 38, 94–95, 172
Bennis, Warren, 20
Block, Peter, 110
Bloom's taxonomy, 34
Business alignment
  organization development interventions and, 14–15, 25, 34
  with organization development projects, 46–54
  V-model, 46–47
Business Ally, 13
Business databases, 73
Business impact. *See also* Isolating the effects
  case studies of, 162–169, 187–188
  data collection, 76
  data regarding, 36, 38, 76
  interventions for, 43–44
  measures of, 49
  objectives, 51, 54
  questionnaires on, 164–169, 185–186
  study, 111
Business needs, 48–49, 52

C

Case studies
  diagnostics, 55–56
  organization culture change, 131–147
  organizational change, 175–195
  stress management, 149–173
Certification, of leaders, 117
Champion, 116
Change
  case study of, 131–147
  definition of, 9
  description of, 3
  desired state of, 9
  keeping pace with, 23
  measurements taken before and after change, 75
  measures of, 36
  preparation for, 10
  reinforcement of, 10
  resistance to, 113–114. See also Resistance
Change agent, 31
Change management
  case study of, 192–193
  metaphor of, 9
  phases of, 9–10
  setting the stage for, 16–17
Checklist, 63
Chief Culture Officer, 27
Clients
  description of, 13
  dissatisfaction of, 89–90
  in feedback process, 110
  reactions of, to data, 110
  recommendations from, 110
  ROI Methodology and, 123
Climate surveys, 99, 116
Closely supervised leadership style, 30
Collaborative environment, 29

Collins, Jim, 28
Communicating results
  audience's opinion, 105
  audience-specific considerations, 102–103
  case study of, 189–192
  communication mode used for, 103
  consistency in, 104
  feedback, 109–111
  hiding of results, 104
  impact study created after, 111
  improvement from, 104
  meetings used for, 107, 110
  neutrality in, 103–104
  overview of, 101
  plan for, 111
  political implications of, 105
  recommendations included in final report, 105
  report used for, 105–107
  routine tools used for, 109
  to senior management, 107–109
  to target audience, 102–103
  testimonials, 104
  timeliness of, 102, 110
Communication and implementation plan, 57
Competencies, 12–13
Confrontation, 110
Control groups, 80, 159–160
Coordinator salary, 96–97
Core values, 29
Costs
  acquisition, 96
  case study of, 170–171
  design and development, 96
  diagnostics, 96
  evaluation, 97
  implementation, 96–97
  needs assessments, 96
  operation and maintenance, 97
  overhead, 97
Credible Activist, 13
Crosby, Phillip, 89
Culture. See Organization culture
Culture and Change Steward, 13
Customer dissatisfaction, 89–90. See also Clients

D

Data
  applications of, 7, 125–126
  business needs arranged in categories of, 49
  negative, 110
  positive, 110
  process improvements by using, 21–22
  qualitative, 61–62
  quantitative, 61–62
  ROI Methodology. See ROI Methodology, data
  simplifying of, 110
  sources of. See Data sources
Data analysis, 79, 184–185
Data collection
  accuracy of, 77, 109
  action plans. See Action plan(s)
  case study of, 160
  in diagnostics, 15
  evaluation method affected by, 42
  focus groups, 66–67
  immediate manager's time for, 76–77
  inclusion of, in process, 20–21
  interviews, 66
  mixed types of, 62
  objectives of, 61
  observations, 67–68
  organization culture influences on, 62
  performance needs identified through, 50
  questionnaires, 62–65, 77, 164–169
  response rate improvements, 73–74
  surveys, 62, 63
  testing, 65
  timing of, 56, 61, 75–77
  work activity disruptions caused by, 77
Data collection plan, 56, 58–59, 123, 136–139, 152–155
Data gathering, 7, 184
Data sources
  business databases, 73
  direct reports, 75
  external groups, 75
  group members' immediate managers, 74–75
  internal groups, 75
  intervention group members, 74–75
  operational databases, 73
  team/peer group, 75
Data-driven decisions, 30
Data-driven organizations, 29
Davidson, Harmon, 17
Decision making, 11
Democratic leadership style, 30
Design and development costs, 96
Diagnosis, data-driven, 7
Diagnostics
  case study of, 55–56
  costs of, 96
  not conducting of, 15–16
  ROI Methodology integration with, 45–46
Direct outputs, monetary value of, 87–88
Direct reports, 75
Diversity, 99–100

E

E-commerce, 24
Employees

collaborative environment for, 29
empowerment of, 28–29
Employment engagement measures, 98–99
Empowered leadership style, 30
Error reduction, 30
Evaluation
behavior change and performance, 42
case studies of, 151–152, 185–189
costs of, 97
data collection influence on method of, 42
determination of, 42
guidelines for, 119, 121
interventions for, 42–43
learning, 42
levels of, 46
organization development initiatives, 41
planning of, 54–55
procedures for, 119, 121
Evaluation targets, 118–119
Expenditures evaluations
benefit-cost ratio, 94–95
payback period for, 94
ROI used for, 93
Expert estimation, 86
Expert opinions, for estimating soft data improvements, 91
External groups, data from, 75
External studies, 91

F
Facility costs, 97
Feedback
action plan for, 109
case study of, 135–136
description of, 7
in high-performing cultures, 29
on reaction questionnaires, 63
Focus groups, 66–67
Follow-up evaluation, 75
Forecasting, 83

G
Globalization, 24
Google, 27
Grievances, 90
Group members
communicating results to, 103
immediate managers of, as data sources, 74–75
Guidelines, 119, 121

H
High-performing organizations, 28–29
Historical costs, 90
Human resources measures, 49–50

I
Impact. See Business impact
Implementation
costs of, 96–97
data, 36
ROI Methodology. See ROI Methodology, implementation of
sustaining of, 35
Information sharing, 30
Information technology, 24
Innovation, 25
Input objectives, 51
Intangible assets, 98
Intangible benefits, 169, 188
Intangible data, 38
Internal groups, data from, 75
Interventions. See also Organization development interventions
for business impact, 43–44
client requirement, 44
cost of, 43
duration of, 43, 45
management interest in, 44
time commitment for, 43–44
unsuitable, for ROI analysis, 44–45
visibility of, 44
Interviews, 66
Invisible observation, 67–68
Isolating the effects, of organization development interventions
description of, 21, 71, 79–80
techniques for
control groups, 80
customer input, 86
expert estimation, 86
forecasting methods, 83
manager's estimation, 85
participant estimation, 83–85
trend-line analysis, 80–83

J
Johari window, 133–134
Joint action planning, 7

K
Kirkpatrick, Don, 46

L
Leader, of ROI process, 117
Leadership
consistency in, 28
empowering style of, 28–30
increased investment in, 24
Level 5, 28
in organization culture, 11, 28

styles of, 30
Learning
ROI process as tool for, 121–122
satisfaction and, 38
testing as method of measuring, 65
Learning data, 36, 64–65
Learning evaluation, 42
Learning needs, 50, 52
Learning objectives, 18, 51
Learning organization, 10
Level 1, 50–52
Level 2, 50, 52
Level 3, 49–50, 52
Level 4, 48–49, 52
Level 5, 28, 48, 52
Lewin, Kurt, 5–6

M

Management
case study of involvement by, 158–159
communicating results to, 102–103, 107–109
lack of support from, 20
ROI Methodology understood by, 34, 108, 123–124
Managers
description of, 13
estimations by, on improvements, 85, 92
group members', data collection from, 74–75
as ROI leader, 117
Materials and supplies costs, 97
Measurement culture
advantages of, 30
building of, 31
Measures
of change, 36
employment engagement, 98–99
organization development initiatives used to establish, 32
organizational commitment, 98–99
reviewing of, 31
timing of, 76
Measuring results, 7
Meetings, communicating results in, 107, 110
Mergers, 17–18
Mixed methodology, 62
Modification step, 7
Monetary value
action plans, 69, 71
case studies of, 169–170, 189
of customer/client dissatisfaction, 89–90
data conversions to, 87–92
of direct outputs, 87–88
of increased output, 87
of quality improvements, 88–90
of rework, 89
of scrap/waste, 89
of soft data, 90–92
of time savings, 88
Multiple-choice question, 63

N

Needs analysis levels
business needs (Level 4), 48–49, 52
learning needs (Level 2), 50, 52
payoff needs (Level 5), 48, 52
performance needs (Level 3), 49–50, 52
preference needs (Level 1), 50–52
Needs assessments
business, 48–49, 52
case study of, 150–151
costs of, 96
learning, 50, 52
payoff, 48, 52
performance, 49–50, 52
preference, 50–52
project evaluation linked with, 51–52

O

Objectives
application, 51
impact, 51, 54
importance of, 18–19
input, 51
learning, 51
levels of, 51, 54
planned action, 51
reaction, 51
ROI, 54
satisfaction, 51
writing of, 18–19
Observations, 67–68
Open-ended question, 63
Operation and maintenance costs, 97
Operational databases, 73
Operational Executor, 13
Organization(s)
collaborative environment in, 29
data-driven, 29
definition of, 13
high-performing, 28–29
learning, 10
Organization culture
climate surveys of, 99
data collection affected by, 62
description of, 10–11
domains used to measure, 11
high-performing, 28–30
lack of understanding about, 17–18
leadership in
description of, 11, 28

styles of, 30
measurement-based, 30–31
mergers affected by lack of understanding about, 17–18
organization effectiveness and, relationship between, 29–30
planning in, 11, 29
Organization culture change
case study of, 131–147
as intangible measure, 99
Organization Designer, 13
Organization development
business case for, 5
challenges for, 23–24
definition of, 4
evaluation of, 22
forecast for, 24–25
practitioners, 12, 31
ROI Methodology and, 31–39. See also ROI Methodology
steps involved in, 5–8
terms associated with, 8–13
Organization development initiatives
activity-based, 32–33
adverse reaction to, 35
evaluation of, 41
perceptions about, 23–24
results-based, 32–33
Organization development interventions. See also Interventions
action plan for. See Action plan
bottom-line results of, 33
business not aligned with, 14–15, 25, 34
chain of impact, 22
consequences of not providing, 95
costs of. See Costs
description of, 7
isolating the effects of. See Isolating the effects, of organization development interventions
return on. See Return, on organization development intervention
types of, 4
value added with, 45
Organization development projects
failure of, 13, 22–23, 122
selection of, 122
Organization development recipient stakeholders, 13
Organization development team
guidelines and procedures developed using input from, 119
measurement and evaluation responsibility of, 118
perspectives of, climate surveys to assess, 116
preparation of, 121
resistance of, to ROI process. See Resistance
ROI implementation participation from, 121
ROI leader on, 117
teaching of, 122
Organization effectiveness
criteria for measuring, 8–9
cultural characteristics associated with, 28–29
measures of, 36
organization culture and, relationship between, 29–30
Organization learning, 10
Organization needs, 15
Organizational change
case study of, 175–195
description of, 3
Organizational commitment measures, 98–99
Organizer salary, 96–97
Output, monetary value of increases in, 87
Overhead costs, 97

P

Participants
estimation by, of improvements, 83–85, 91–92
salaries and benefits for, 97
Payback period, 94
Payoff needs, 48, 52
Peer group, data from, 75
Performance agreements, 68
Performance needs, 49–50, 52
Pitfalls
change management, 16–17
data collection not built into process, 20–21
diagnostics not conducted, 15–16
failure to identify behavior, 18–19
intervention effects not isolated, 21
lack of business alignment, 14–15
organization culture not understood, 17–18
right people not included in process, 19
Planned action objectives, 51
Planning
of evaluation, 54–55
in organization culture, 11, 29
Post-intervention testing, 65
Preference needs, 50–52
Pre-intervention testing, 65
Preliminary assessment step, 7
Preliminary evaluation, 7
Procedures, 119, 121
Process improvement, 21–22
Profit, time savings effect on, 88
Progress tracking, 30
Project cost data, 35

Q

Qualitative data, 61–62

Quality, costs of, 90
Quality improvements, 88–90
Quantitative data, 61–62
Questionnaires, 62–65, 77, 164–169, 185–186

R
Ranking scale, 63
Reaction data, 36–37, 41, 65
Reaction evaluation, 42
Reaction objectives, 51
Reaction questionnaire, 63
Refreezing, 6, 35
Report, for communicating results, 105–107
Resistance
  minimizing of, 113–114
  overcoming of
  description of, 114–116
  roles and responsibilities developed for, 116–118
  types of, 115
Response rates, 21
Results
  communicating. See Communicating results
  hiding of, 104
  measuring of, 7
Results-based initiatives, 32–33
Return, on organization development intervention
  benefit-cost ratio, 94–95
  calculation of, 92–95
  payback period for, 94
Rework, monetary value of, 89
ROI
  data on, 38
  definition of, 35, 92–93
  expenditures evaluations using, 93
  formula for calculating, 92–93, 172
  sustaining the use of, 113–114
ROI analysis
  data sources for, 73–75
  interventions for, 41–45
  planning for, 54–55
  project selection for, 122
ROI analysis plan, 56, 60, 123, 137, 140, 154, 156
ROI Methodology
  business needs, 15
  chain of impact, 21–22
  champion of, 116
  client preparations, 123
  data
  behavior change and implementation, 36–37
  business impact, 36–38
  categories of, 37
  intangible, 38
  learning, 36–37
  overview of, 34–35
  project cost, 35, 37
  reaction, 36–37, 41
  ROI, 37–38
data collection, 21
diagnostics integrated with, 45–46
discussion groups on, 123
environments and projects, 35
executive preparations, 123–124
history of, 33–34
implementation of
  consistency in, 114
  efficiency in, 114
  guidelines and procedures development and revision, 119, 121
  importance of, 114
  leader for, 117
  organization development team involvement in, 121
  plan for, 119–120
  roles and responsibilities developed for, 116–118
  task force for, 117
leader of, 117
as learning tool, 121–122
management's understanding of, 34, 108, 123–124
myths regarding, 124–125
objections to, 115
obstacles to, 124
organization development and, 31–39
Process Model, 38–39
projects for showing value of
  bad news from, 125
  data from, 125–126
  discussion groups, 123
  obstacles to, 124
  planning documents used in, 123
  progress monitoring, 123, 126
  selection of, 122
  rationale for, 33–34
  resistance to. See Resistance
  senior management's understanding of, 34, 108, 123–124
ROI objectives, 54
Roles and responsibilities, for ROI process implementation, 116–118

S
Salaries, 96–97
Satisfaction
  learning and, 38
  objectives, 51
Senge, Peter, 10
Senior management

communicating results to, 102–103, 107–109
meeting with, 108
ROI Methodology understood by, 34, 108
Service
poor, market damage caused by, 90
time savings effect on, 88
Soft data, monetary value of, 90–92
Stakeholders
chain of impact understood by, 38
description of, 12–13
reaction data from, 36
ROI outcomes and, 34
Strategic initiatives, 43
Strategy Architect, 13
Stress management, 149–173
Stress reduction, 100
Structured interview, 66
Supervisors, 103
Surveys, 62, 63

T

Talent Manager, 13
Tangible assets, 98
Task force, 117
Team group, data from, 75
Team-based process, for product development, 52
Testimonials, 104
Testing, data collection through, 65
360-degree feedback, 6, 55, 67
Time savings, monetary value of, 88
Travel expenses, 97
Trend-line analysis, 80–83
Two-way question, 63

U

Unfreezing, 5–6, 113
Unnoticeable observation, 68
Unstructured interview, 66
Urgency, 16

V

V-Model
alignment with, 46–47
needs assessment linked with project evaluation, 51–52

W

Workforce, globalization effects on, 24

HOW TO PURCHASE ASTD PRESS PRODUCTS

All ASTD Press titles may be purchased through ASTD's online store at **www.store.astd.org**.

ASTD Press products are available worldwide through various outlets and booksellers. In the United States and Canada, individuals may also purchase titles (print or e-book) from:

Amazon– www.amazon.com (USA); www.amazon.com (CA)
Google Play– play.google.com/store
EBSCO– www.ebscohost.com/ebooks/home

Outside the United States, English-language ASTD Press titles may be purchased through distributors (divided geographically).

United Kingdom, Continental Europe, the Middle East, North Africa, Central Asia, and Latin America:
Eurospan Group
Phone: 44.1767.604.972
Fax: 44.1767.601.640
Email: eurospan@turpin-distribution.com
Web: www.eurospanbookstore.com
For a complete list of countries serviced via Eurospan please visit www.store.astd.org or email publications@astd.org.

South Africa:
Knowledge Resources
Phone: +27(11)880-8540
Fax: +27(11)880-8700/9829
Email: mail@knowres.co.za
Web: http://www.kr.co.za
For a complete list of countries serviced via Knowledge Resources please visit www.store.astd.org or email publications@astd.org.

Nigeria:
Paradise Bookshops
Phone: 08033075133
Email: paradisebookshops@gmail.com
Website: www.paradisebookshops.com

Asia:
Cengage Learning Asia Pte. Ltd.
Email: asia.info@cengage.com
Web: www.cengageasia.com
For a complete list of countries serviced via Cengage Learning please visit www.store.astd.org or email publications@astd.org.

India:
Cengage India Pvt. Ltd.
Phone: 011 43644 1111
Fax: 011 4364 1100
Email: asia.infoindia@cengage.com

For all other countries, customers may send their publication orders directly to ASTD. Please visit: **www.store.astd.org**.